WALKING TO
THE PROMISED LAND

Lori Belihar Boyd

ISBN-10: 1944704280
ISBN-13: 978-1944704285

Library of Congress Control Number: 2017932386

Published by Start2Finish
Fort Worth, Texas 76244
www.start2finish.org

Printed in the United States of America

Cover Design: Josh Feit, Evangela.com

To my dad, Robert Belihar,

who continues to teach me how to walk.

I love you.

TABLE OF
CONTENTS

FOREWORD

ROBERT P. BELIHAR, MS, MD, MPH

Brigadier General, USAF (Ret.)
Nashville, Tennessee

You're holding in your hands a book that will undoubtedly have a positive effect on your life, perhaps even profoundly so. *Walking to the Promised Land* is a beautifully written, informative work that is presented in a user friendly format. Beethoven took a simple four note motive and created a masterpiece, his Fifth Symphony. In like fashion Lori, the author and my daughter, has chosen a simple theme and created a marvelous work of great worth and lasting significance. I admit the use of hyperbole here, but as a proud father, that's the way I see it. *Walking to the Promised Land* was a labor of love. It is the product of a great deal of effort and collaboration. It is an informative, thought provoking resource to aid in your journey and is a great addition to any library. Its content and format make it an excellent resource for Bible studies and other venues.

From the beginning of time man has pondered the question "Why am I here?" The answer is clearly stated in Ecclesiastes 12:12: *"Fear God and keep His commandments for this is the whole duty of man."* Man, created by God, was not left to flounder. Through his Word, the Bible, God has made clear his will. The Scriptures serve as a roadmap for your journey here on earth with the Promised Land (Heaven) as your destination. God's plan for you is laid out with elegant simplicity in his Word. *Walking to the Promised Land* serves as an excellent travel guide to aid in dealing with life's challenges along the way that may distract, deter, or disrupt your progress toward our heavenly home.

During my nearly forty-eight years of practicing medicine, I have always placed emphasis on prevention; I encourage my patients to embrace a healthy lifestyle and walk a wellness path that will lead them to better quality of life and a longer lifespan. Good stewardship does have its reward. However, as we all know, in spite of your best efforts, your body's destiny is certain. Being mortal, it eventually wears out and must return to the earth from whence it came. *"The dust returns to the earth as it was, and the spirit returns to God who gave it."* (Ecclesiastes 12:7). Walking the road to wellness is being a good steward of your fleshly body, which is temporal. However, more importantly, walking to the Promised Land is being a good steward of your soul, which is eternal.

The author has done a masterful job in organizing her material for maximum benefit to you, the reader. Her goal is for you to become more intentional in your daily spiritual walk. You make a broad range of choices every day of your life and that includes how you will live for Christ each day. *Walking* is sure to stimulate self-examination, provide a better understanding of what is at stake, empower you to make the difficult choices, and enable you to lead a more meaningful life that culminates in your entrance one day into the Promised Land.

——

DR. BELIHAR *has been certified by the American Boards of Preventive Medicine (Sub-specialty Aerospace Medicine), Anti-Aging Medicine, and Ophthalmology. In addition to the Doctor of Medicine Degree, he has been awarded the Degrees of Master of Science and Master of Public Health. He completed a highly successful career in the United States Air Force, retiring with the rank of Brigadier General. During his tour in the military, he held a wide range of positions, ranging from squadron flight surgeon to Command Surgeon at United States Central Command under Gen. H. Norman Schwarzkopf. While serving as CENTCOM Surgeon, he oversaw the establishment of a healthcare system for over 500,000 deployed personnel during Desert Shield/ Desert Storm, including preparations for the enemy's potential use of chemical and biological agents. At the time of his retirement from the USAF, Gen. Belihar was Commander of the Human Systems Center (HSC), Commander of Brooks Air Force Base, and Commandant of the USAF School of Aerospace Medicine. As commander of HSC, he had oversight of an organization of nearly 4,000* *personnel, whose mission was dedicated to human performance enhancement, including participation in the development and management of the Air Force wellness and fitness programs.*

Dr. Belihar currently serves as the Medical Director of the CareHere Health-Signs Center in Brentwood, TN, a medical practice that centers upon comprehensive health assessment in conjunction with lifestyle management as the primary approach to disease management and healthy aging. Widely traveled, he has visited 71 countries. Touched by the suffering he has witnessed in the Third World, he has often served as a medical missionary overseas. He and his wife, Anita, reside in Nashville, TN. They have three children and eight grandchildren.

ACKNOWLEDGEMENTS

The compiling of this book has been a journey in itself. As with every writing project, this one had bumps and turns, but the destination was worth the ride because I'm a better traveler now than before I began. I pray that you will find the same to be true as you work through each chapter of this Bible study.

When the idea for *Walking to the Promised Land* began to take shape in my mind I knew that it had to be written into book format, and I am grateful for the people who helped make it happen:

My husband, Sam Boyd, and our three children, Evie, Kate, and Briggs, who make every day of this life-journey exciting and wonderful. They beautify my wilderness in the biggest and smallest of ways. I can't imagine walking to the Promised Land without these four sojourners by my side. We keep each other moving in the right direction!

My Dad, Dr. Robert Belihar, the smartest man I know, whose love for learning and for helping people has always inspired me to want to be my best and do my best. He tells me he loves me and that he's proud of me every chance he gets—words that have cultivated a lifetime of ambition in the heart of this girl. He is a hero of a father. His knowledge and expertise in the areas of health and wellness are reflected in the "Walk with the Doc" section you'll find at the end of every chapter.

My sister, Jennifer Belihar Richardson, who amazes me with her talent, creativity, and wisdom. I've always looked up to her, from the days of Jon Bon Jovi posters and big hair to the days of Sippy-cups and SUVs. She is strong and beautiful. As an exercise physiologist, she developed the walking charts and plans that are included in the appendix of this book, as well as the Take Action challenges.

My mom, Anita Belihar, my sister Julia Belihar Battles, my friends, and the precious sisters I have met at ladies' events all over the world who support me and show me such kindness and love. I am thankful for each of you.

My editor and kindred spirit, Kristy Hinson, whose wisdom and incredible talent has made this book better. I love her for her kindness, for her honesty, but most of all for her beautiful, Christ-like heart.

My publisher and friend, Michael Whitworth, whose patience and encouragement continue to be such a blessing to me. His faith motivates and edifies unpretentiously. I am thankful that our paths crossed and even more thankful for the kingdom work he does so passionately and selflessly.

I'm happy that you're holding this book in your hands, and my sincere hope is that this study will be a blessing to you. I pray that the lessons will bring purpose and focus to your daily spiritual walk and that God will be glorified with every step you take.

INTRODUCTION

THEN...

*E*den looked at the horizon and although she could no longer see the sun, its prevailing light had not yet surrendered to night fall. The distant mountains rose up as black shadows against the deep blue sky. *But darkness was coming.* Today marked the fourteenth day, and it was time. She knew the instructions, she had rehearsed the plan in her head over and over for the past four days, yet as she looked down at her trembling hands she could not deny her fear.

Standing in the doorway of her home, she could hear her husband behind her talking to their children once more about the things that would happen before the sun rose again. *How could he know what to say?* She knew in her heart that no one knew what the next hour would bring, much less the next morning.

Taking a deep breath, Eden turned to face her family. Titus, on his knees, had drawn their three children into his arms and was gently kissing the tops of their heads. He whispered something into their ears that Eden could not hear, but it seemed to bring smiles to the three tear-streaked faces.

Then the whole assembly of the congregation shall kill it at twilight. Four days ago Titus had brought the lamb to their home; and now the words of Moses echoed inside her head as he stood and prepared to carry out what had been commanded. Eden walked to the table where she had placed a basin and a bunch of hyssop. As Titus passed by, she handed him the bowl that would soon be filled with the blood of the lamb.

Dip the hyssop into the blood and apply it to the doorposts and to the lintel of your house. Why did the lamb's blood have to mark the doorway? Why was all of this happening on this day and at this time? Why didn't God simply carry out this final plague on the Egyptians without requiring anything from the Israelites? She did not understand the reason for the Lord's instructions, but she knew that she would do anything to save the life of her oldest child, and she trusted the way God had chosen.

The blood will be a sign for you on the houses where you are. And when I see the blood, I will pass over you: and the plague will not be on you to destroy you when I strike the land of Egypt. Those were the words of the Lord, and she had seen with her own eyes God's mighty power at work through the nine terrifying plagues. With each plague, the God of Heaven had silenced the gods of the Egyptians by controlling the source of their presumed deity. He defeated Hapi, god of the Nile, when he turned the water into blood. He conquered Heqet, goddess of birth and fertility, depicted as a woman with the head of a frog, when he infested the land with her likeness. He vanquished the Egyptian god of the sun, Ra, when he filled the land with darkness for three days. And now, with this tenth plague, God would reach out his hand against Pharaoh himself; a man considered by his nation to be a living god, and would strike down the firstborn throughout all of Egypt. Eden thought about Pharaoh's oldest son; she thought about the child's mother and the suffering that would befall even those within the walls of the palace before morning.

Then roast the lamb in fire—its head, its legs, and all of its entrails—and eat it with unleavened bread and bitter herbs. Any of it that is left over should be burned; none of it should remain by morning. Titus brought her the lamb to prepare just as she was placing the dough for their bread onto the table. He took the hyssop, along with the basin, and walked through the front door to apply the blood to the doorposts and lintel of their home. As Eden stoked the fire, she wondered where they would be the following year when the same meal would be eaten as a memorial of this very night. Moses had called it the Lord's Passover and had said that it would be observed as a part of a seven-day feast—the Feast of Unleavened Bread. Moses had told them that all of Israel would observe it as a law to remember how the Lord passed over the houses of the children of Israel and delivered them from death. These thoughts gave Eden some comfort because they spoke of the future and they gave her hope.

Eat quickly, with a belt on your waist, your sandals on your feet, and your staff in your hand. It was clear that they were to be ready to travel. When the word came, they would walk. Their family was dressed and shoes were strapped tightly around each pair of feet. Eden had pulled their robes up and secured the bottom edge beneath the belts fastened around their waists. She looked at Titus, who held his staff firmly in his hand and carried on his shoulders their clothing and other household possessions. They ate in silence. When they had finished, Eden placed all of the leftover food into the fire…and then they waited.

Beginning at midnight cries could be heard throughout the land. Every firstborn tasted death in Egypt, from the firstborn of the Pharaoh to the firstborn of the livestock. Eden's arms held her oldest child so close that she could feel the rise and fall of his chest against her own and tears ran from her eyes. She pictured the blood of the lamb around the door of their home; she recounted how she had roasted the lamb and how she had burned all that remained after they ate; she reviewed all that Moses had said: *Had they done everything they had been told?*

The apathetic hours passed, until finally, while darkness still covered the land, there was a pounding on the door. "It's time! We are free!" Titus gathered his family into an embrace and turning his head upward he cried out, "Praise the God of Heaven!" As he led them toward the door, Eden saw her kneading bowl among the clothes strapped on Titus' back and remembered the dough she had left on the table. She quickly wrapped it in a piece of cloth, recalling that it had not yet been leavened.

Walking down the path that would lead her family out of Goshen, Eden's emotions wrestled within her heart. She felt relief and fear; she felt joy and apprehension; she felt pride and sorrow; but there was one feeling that rose above all the others—the feeling of hope. She had hope for tomorrow, hope for the next day, and for every day thereafter because she had faith in the God of her people, the Israelites. She didn't know what lay ahead, but she did know that the blood of the lamb had saved them, that they were no longer slaves to the Egyptians, and that their journey was just beginning. The Land of Promise awaited, but it would take much walking to get there.

...AND NOW

The story of the Israelites' first Passover and their departure from the land of Egypt can be found in the twelfth chapter of Exodus. It's a story of judgment that results in grief for some and triumph for others. While it is a story that demonstrates the power of God and the importance of obeying his commands, it is also very much a story about the faithful love of God and how he saves his people by grace. Like so many other stories we read on the pages of our Bibles, this one teaches us about our own faith and provides us with important lessons that we can apply to our spiritual lives.

Pharaoh refused to let God's people leave the land of Egypt. God had struck the Egyptians with nine plagues, and the time for the tenth and most devastating plague was at hand: the death of the firstborn. God had a plan to spare the children of Israel from the horror of this plague, but they had to do exactly as he commanded.

There were specific guidelines the children of Israel were to follow as they prepared an unblemished lamb whose blood would be used to mark their homes on the night of the Passover. They were to roast the lamb, not boil it, and they were to burn any part that remained uneaten before morning. The blood of the lamb was to be placed on the doorposts as well as the lintel and would be a sign for the Lord. When the Lord saw the blood of the Lamb, he would pass over the house, and the firstborn child living there would be saved from death, as the land of Egypt suffered through the final plague.

In Exodus 12:11, we read about what God expected of the Israelites as they ate the lamb, *"Now you shall eat it in this manner: with your loins girded, your sandals on your feet, and your staff in your hand; and you shall eat it in haste—it is the Lord's Passover."*

The blood of the lamb would save them and after that they would need to be prepared to walk! They were dressed, with shoes on, staves in hand, and ready to immediately start the journey that would lead them to the Promised Land. There were specific steps they had to take in order to be saved by the blood, but their story did not end there. They had much walking to do! God saved them from the plague of death, he would save while they wandered through the wilderness, and he would save them as they crossed over into the land of Canaan, but they had to obey him...and they had to walk.

The same is true for God's children today. The question we must each ask ourselves is, *"Am I a walking Christian?"* Now that I've been saved by the blood of the perfect lamb, Jesus Christ, have I found a nice comfortable place to sit and kick up my feet, or have I started the journey that, while characterized by a great deal of walking, will ultimately lead me to the Promised Land? Have I fastened on the belt of Truth? Have I strapped the Gospel of peace to my feet? Have I firmly taken a hold of Jesus, like a staff in hand, to help me maneuver the ups and downs of wilderness terrain?

WALKING WITH PURPOSE

It's not enough for us to have a destination in mind and a desire to get there, we must walk! We have to walk with purpose and with determination, but the devil isn't going to make it easy. He's going to discourage us by filling the wilderness with threats and dangers, or he'll create an oasis as delightful as possible to lure us in and keep us from moving ahead. It takes strength to resist the temptations and to keep walking. Sometimes, though, the wilderness is difficult because that's the nature of the wilderness. Life can be hard; it can be cruel even. In those times, when our sorrow tells us to push away, it takes faith to reach for the Father's hand and keep walking, trusting that God is always present and feels the pain of his children.

I took a random poll not too long ago and asked people what they thought was the greatest challenge to daily Christian living. The overwhelming answer was "time." Most of the responders said that the day goes by so quickly that before they know it, it's time for bed and they've not done anything to strengthen their relationship with God, grow their faith, or share Jesus Christ with someone else. We have to decide to make our spiritual lives a priority.

The goal of this study is to help us become intentional in our daily spiritual walk. We make choices every day of our lives. We choose when to wake up, what to wear, what we eat, how we will respond to people, and what we will do for exercise. We also choose how we will live for Christ each day. We can *choose* how we will walk!

The chapters of this book are formatted in the same way. Each chapter features a Scripture that mentions one aspect of our spiritual walk and begins with a discussion about the meaning of that particular aspect, followed by these sections:

A WALKING WARRIOR
An example of a person in the Bible who walked *well*

IN HIS STEPS
A glimpse at how Jesus walked *perfectly*

OUR DAILY WALK
How to incorporate aspects of spiritual walking into our lives on a day-to-day basis

S-T-E-P
How to foster Strength, face Trials, find Encouragement, and remain faithful in Prayer as it relates to our spiritual walk

WALK WITH THE DOC
A walking tip with corresponding information from Dr. Robert Belihar that draws a connection between the spiritual and the physical

TAKE ACTION!
A challenge for your physical health…and for fun!

I pray that this study will be a blessing to you. Stay straight, step sure, and enjoy the journey!

CHAPTER ONE
WILDERNESS WALKING
Trust, Delight, and Commit

"Trust in the Lord, and do good; dwell in the land, and feed on His faithfulness. Delight yourself also in the Lord, and He shall give you the desires of your heart. Commit your way to the Lord, trust also in Him, and He shall bring it to pass." (Psalm 37:3-5)

Several years ago, our family had loaded up the Expedition and headed out for a summer vacation at the beach. The drive from Middle Tennessee to the Carolina coast would take around eleven hours, so we knew we had quite a day ahead! When we had been on the road for about thirty minutes, I remember one of kids yelling from the back seat, *"Are we almost there?"* Sam and I looked at each other in silent dread and mutual awareness that this would be the longest trip ever. It was downhill from there. Shortly after the foreboding question, we had to make a bathroom stop, then a few exits later we pulled over to clean up a carsick child, and several miles after that we said good-bye to a flip-flop that had been tossed out of window along Interstate 24. All of this happened within the first hour of our road trip! Sam and I wondered more than once during those sixty minutes if it would have been better had we just stayed home!

When the Israelites left Egypt, they had no idea how much time they would spend in the wilderness. I wonder how they felt by the end of the first day?...the first week?...the first month? I'm sure the question, *"Are we almost there?"* echoed over and over in the minds of the people. They were not accustomed to travel, much less perpetual camping through a vast wilderness! It's important to remember that the Israelite people had been slaves in the land of Egypt for hundreds of years. When they walked out of Goshen on the night of the final plague, they weren't just leaving their bondage behind, they were leaving their homes, their routines, and the only way of life they had ever known. It was this tug of their familiar past, even though it was a past characterized by oppression, which caused them to continually cry out to Moses saying, *"Why did you bring us out of Egypt? It would have been better for us to stay and serve the Egyptians!"*

It was difficult for God's people to focus on the Promised Land while they were facing obstacles immediately in front of them in the wilderness. It must have been hard to picture a land flowing with milk and honey when their children were crying out in hunger. It's easy to read the stories of the Israelites throughout their wilderness wanderings and get frustrated with their lack of faith, but when you put yourself in their sandals, when you imagine yourself in the Wilderness of Shur or the Wilderness of Sin, with no food, no water, extreme heat, the threat of attack, and no end in sight; it can be perspective changing. In fact, we can learn a great deal about ourselves when we look closely at what life must have been like for God's people in the wilderness.

There are a few Scriptures that paint a picture of the land traveled by the Israelites on their way to Canaan, and the images are grim:

"So we departed from Horeb, and went through all that great and terrible wilderness which you saw on the way to the mountains of the Amorites, as the Lord our God had commanded us. Then we came to Kadesh Barnea" (Deuteronomy 1:19).

"When your heart is lifted up and you forget the Lord your God who brought you out of the land of Egypt, from the house of bondage; who led you through that great and terrible wilderness, in which were fiery serpents and scorpions and thirsty land where there was no water; who brought water for you out of the flinty rock" (Deuteronomy 8:14-15).

In Jeremiah 2:6, the Lord spoke these words to the prophet, *"Neither did they say, 'Where is the Lord, who brought us up out of the land of Egypt, who led us through the wilderness, through a land of deserts and pits, through a land of drought and the shadow of death, through a land that no one crossed and where no one dwelt?'"*

The wilderness terrain was arduous. Mountains rose above the rocks and sand, under the shroud of unrelenting heat. The ground was difficult to navigate and dangers threatened from all around. But it wasn't just the terrain that made the wilderness *"great and terrible."* We can read accounts found in Exodus 15, 17, and Numbers 20 about the lack of water and in Exodus 16 and Numbers 11 about the lack of food. We know that there were enemies that the Israelites encountered on their journey (Exodus 17, Numbers 14, 21) and there was an incessant lure to worship false gods when they were faced with challenges (Exodus 32, Numbers 25).

In Goshen, the Israelites lived under the rule of a pharaoh who cared nothing for them. They worked and suffered at the hands of the Egyptians, but God heard their cries. He loved them, saved them, and would lead them through the wilderness to the land he had promised Abraham. To the Israelites, the wilderness meant freedom; but it also meant opposition and struggle. It meant slipping out of the ease of bondage and stepping into trials of faith. The wilderness was foreboding and threatening, but God was there! He would take care of them, but they would have to trust him and obey his commands. If they did that, they would experience the joy of their Promised Land. In Egypt they might have had some comforts, but in the wilderness they had hope!

Our Present-day Wilderness

Today, as children of God, we are also on a journey to our Promised Land. The journey begins when we are washed by the blood of the perfect Lamb through baptism, saved from the bondage of sin, and it will end at the gates of Heaven. But, between the beginning and the end, there is a wilderness to endure. Just as the Israelites stood on the bank of the Red Sea, with the enemies of their former life behind them and the wilderness outstretched before them, we come through the water with a choice to make. *Do we keep walking?*

Our wilderness is not characterized by rocks, sand, and mountains; instead it is made up of the trials and struggles, the joys and triumphs that define this life on earth. Our threats may not come in the form of heat or rugged terrain, but they do come in the form of illness, stress, heartbreak, and temptation. Our wilderness today is life itself, with all of its jubilant highs and devastating lows. The path can be hard and the walking is not always easy. The devil stands ready to attack and the danger of sin is everywhere. There are idols fighting for our time and attention. Like the wilderness, life is impartial to its company—it doesn't hold back sand storms or scorpions depending on the traveler—everyone endures its desolation and faces its perils.

We will hunger and we will thirst. Like the Israelites, we might even long for the days of bondage: when it was easy to live with the conveniences and pleasures of sin. We might find an oasis, like in the Wilderness of Elim, and really want to stay there, giving up the ultimate reward for temporary happiness. *Do we keep walking?*

My mother-in-law tells a story about when my husband, Sam, started Kindergarten. He jumped out of the bed on the first day completely filled with excitement and ready to go! On the second day, he woke right up, still happy about going to his new school. But by the third day, she had to drag him out of his bed while he cried out, *"How long does this go on!"*

We will be discouraged at times, and we will want to quit, but we keep walking! We keep walking because God is with us! We keep walking because he has shown us the way! We keep walking because even though the wilderness is foreboding and threatening, we catch glimpses of God's glory everyday and everywhere. There are days we will look to the sky and cry out, *"How long does this go on?"* But we keep walking because God has promised Heaven to his faithful children, and God keeps his promises!

God is Present and He Provides

One of the amazing and wonderful things about the story of the Israelites' journey through the wilderness is that God's Providence can be seen over and over again. He provided for them in their hunger and in their thirst, he provided for them through the leadership of Moses, and he provided for them by His guidance through a cloud by day and a fire by night. He demonstrated his power through signs and miracles, he protected them in battles and against illness, and when the tabernacle had been constructed, he lived among them there.

The wilderness, in all of its dread and uncertainty, was a place for the Israelites to draw near to God. It was a place for them to witness his divine authority and come to understand his compassion and love. Through their wilderness journey, the children of Israel had an opportunity to deepen their relationship with God and to increase their faith as they depended on him for survival. He was showing them the way; all they had to do was follow him in obedience. It's sad to learn from Scripture that the Israelites disappointed God time after time because of their lack of faith. Instead of discovering spiritual renewal while in the vast wilderness, they fell victim to doubt, fear, and hopelessness, which led to forty years of wandering and ultimately kept a generation of Israelites from ever reaching the Promised Land. I heard it said once that "It took God one night to get Israel out of Egypt, but it took forty years to get Egypt out of Israel."

God continues to show us his Providence in the way he cares for us today. Through his Son, Jesus Christ, he has offered us the bread of life and provided us a way to salvation. Through the church, he has brought us into his family as his children. Through prayer, he has allowed us to personally approach his throne of grace with our petitions, our confessions, our praise, and our gratitude. Through the Bible, he has given us a guide for our steps as we walk daily through this life. His Word is now our cloud by day and fire by night! It's what we follow so that we can navigate through the wilderness and reach our Promised Land. God still works in our lives, in his time, in his way, and always for the purpose of accomplishing his will. We have to trust him, especially when the wilderness seems vicious and unrelenting. It's in those times that he's making us stronger sojourners—sojourners who can help others through their own wilderness journeys and who will walk as faithful testimonies to his goodness and glory.

Footsteps in the Sand

The journey of the Israelites through the wilderness was one that required physical walking. It involved daily activity, miles of stepping through the sands of the desert, and the interaction of every system of the body. Their human selves were put to the test just as their spiritual selves were tested.

In the book of Deuteronomy, we have the record of Moses' final messages to the new generation of Israelites who would enter the Promised Land. It is a book about how God has dealt with his people—what he has done for them in the past, what he expects of them in the present, and what he will do for them in the future. Moses reminded them repeatedly of the ways God had taken care of them during their time in the wilderness:

"For the Lord your God has blessed you in all the work of your hand. He knows your trudging through this great wilderness. These forty years the Lord your God has been with you; you have lacked nothing" (Deuteronomy 2:7).

"Now this is the commandment, and these are the statutes and judgments which the Lord your God has commanded to teach you, that you may observe them in the land which you are crossing over to possess, that you fear the Lord your God, to keep all His statutes and His commandments which I command you, you and your son and your grandson, all the days of your life, and that your days may be prolonged. Therefore, hear, O Israel, and be careful to observe it, that it may be well with you, and that you may multiply greatly as the Lord God of your fathers has promised you—'a land flowing with milk and honey" (Deuteronomy 6:1-3).

In Deuteronomy 8:4, Moses reminded the people, *"Your garments did not wear out on you, nor did your foot swell these forty years."*

When it came to the threat of war, Moses told them, *"...Hear O Israel: Today you are on the verge of battle with your enemies. Do not let your heart faint, do not be afraid, and do not tremble or be terrified because of them; for the Lord your God is He who goes with you, to fight for you against your enemies, to save you"* (Deuteronomy 20:3-4).

God took care of his people mentally, physically, *and* spiritually.

The mind, body, and spirit connection is strong. The three interweave and work together to create our state of being. When there is a balance between the mind, body, and spirit, we can experience wellness and find peace. It's easy to see how this happens! Think about how your level of stress affects your sleep, which affects your energy, which affects your mood, which affects your relationships with others. The way we think, and what we do, influences who we are! Attitude determines behavior, behavior determines habits, and habits determine character.

When we are mindful of how our spirit is affected by our thinking and our actions, we can make a conscious effort to strengthen each part of our being to achieve better health overall. *Walking to the Promised Land* is a study that draws a relationship between physical walking and spiritual walking. This study not only considers the analogies between the actual wilderness traveled by the Israelites and the spiritual wilderness we experience today, but it also examines how physical walking can teach us important lessons about how to daily walk as a Christian throughout this life.

Footsteps of the Spirit

I've mentioned already how God has taken care of us by providing his Word as a guide for our journey through life. He has given us the road map, and he has promised us Heaven, but it's up to us to do the walking. Never fear! God has told us exactly how we should walk in order to conquer the wilderness, and he has assured us that he will be with us every step of the way. As he led the footsteps of the Israelites through the sands of the desert, so he leads our spiritual footsteps today.

There are many verses in the Bible that describe the kind of walking that should be characteristic of a Christian. These "walking verses" refer to our spiritual walk, or in other words, the manner in which we live as disciples of Christ. Reading and studying these passages will help us as we navigate through this life—our own individual wilderness. Throughout the course of this study, we are going to look at some of the "walking verses" and learn how we can become more intentional in our daily spiritual living. Baptism is the beginning, the starting point of this journey, and what follows is a life of faithful walking as we travel the road that will take us to Heaven.

A WALKING WARRIOR

If we're going to talk about someone in the Bible who was a warrior when it came to wilderness walking, we have to talk about Moses. We know him best as the baby in the basket who was "drawn out of the water" by Pharaoh's daughter and who would later lead his people, the Hebrews, out of slavery in Egypt, through the wilderness, and to the land God had promised Abraham. But I want to talk about a phase of Moses' life that is often overlooked. I want us to think about the "pre-wilderness" wilderness walking he did in the middle of his life—the forty years of his life that fall between the first forty, which were lived as a prince in the palace of the pharaoh, and the last forty, which were lived as a sojourner in the wilderness.

Moses grew up as an Egyptian royal, living a life of privilege and wealth. We know from Stephen's address to the Jewish council in Acts 7:22 that Moses had been educated in all the wisdom of the Egyptians and was mighty in words and deeds. Despite the leadership and fame that would certainly be his under the powerful arm of Pharaoh, Moses' heart was with his people, the Hebrew slaves.

When he was forty years old, he witnessed an Egyptian beating one of his Hebrew brothers, and being unable to stand by and do nothing, Moses defended and avenged the slave by killing the Egyptian and burying his body in the sand. He thought that God would use him to deliver the Hebrews at that time, and he thought that the Hebrews would understand that, but they did not understand; Moses' timing did not match up with God's timing. Word spread about what he had done, and it eventually fell upon the ears of Pharaoh. Moses' life was then in danger, and he ran.

He ran to a far away place called Midian, situated in the wilderness, a home to herdsmen and livestock. When Moses reached the city, he sat down by a well and soon noticed seven sisters who had come to water their father's flock. While he was watching them, a group of shepherds came and began to drive the women away. Moses came to their rescue and helped them fill their troughs with water. Later that day, when the sisters told their father what had happened at the well, Moses was invited to come eat with them. He stayed for much longer than one meal! Moses ended up living with their family and married Zipporah, one of the daughters of Jethro. He became a father of two sons and lived for forty years in the wilderness of Midian as a shepherd until one day on Mount Horeb, he saw a bush unlike any other.

The forty years Moses spent in Midian were not wasted years. They were years of preparation. They were years of purpose. They were threads in the tapestry of Moses' life, each year woven by the gentle hand of the providential God. Moses had lessons to learn, and God had plans to fulfill…in His perfect time.

Caring for the weak and the oppressed

We read in Acts 7:23 something about the heart of Moses. That verse tells us that when Moses was forty years old, "it came into his heart to visit his brethren, the children of Israel." Moses knew who he was, and he knew that it was his people who were being forced to live in slavery. He had to see them; and when he saw one of them suffering, he had to do something. Killing the Egyptian was impulsive and wrong, but we see evidence of a tender spot in the heart of Moses for the weak and the oppressed. The next day, when he saw two Israelites fighting, he tried to reconcile them. He didn't want to see his brothers mistreating each other. This paints another picture of Moses' concern for others. Then, shortly after arriving in Midian, he stood up for Jethro's daughters when they were being bullied by a group of shepherds. Time after time, we see that Moses genuinely cared about people.

His spirit of compassion evolved into something even more when he became a shepherd. He learned how to care for and nurture a flock of sheep that could not help themselves. He learned how to protect them. He learned how to feed them and how to quench their thirst. He learned how to heal them, how to shear them, how to rescue them, and how to provide them with rest. Moses learned how to gently and lovingly shepherd sheep because one day God would use him to gently and lovingly shepherd a nation.

Learning the ways of the wilderness

While living in Midian, which was situated in the middle of the Arabian desert, Moses became accustomed to wilderness living. Those years were valuable because they provided him with knowledge that would later translate to wisdom as he led God's people through the same terrain on their way to Canaan.

Imagine all the new things Moses had to learn! His new life in Midian was in complete contrast to life in Egypt. He became a tent-dweller, a sheep herder, a husband, a father, and the son-in-law of a priest. He had to walk long distances in the heat, over difficult terrain, and with little water. With every callous, every blister, every sunburn, every moment of thirst, every drop of sweat, and every sundown met with exhaustion, Moses was learning important lessons in wilderness living. Those lessons were not without purpose. God was using them to build a leader who had the experience and ability to walk confidently out of Egypt with a nation behind him and a vast wilderness ahead.

Developing a spirit of humility

From living as a prince in an Egyptian palace to working as a shepherd in the wilderness, Moses learned humility. From a life of privilege to a life a servitude, Moses learned submission. From believing himself to be the deliverer of the Israelite nation to falling on his feet forty years later in front of a burning bush and asking, "Who am I that I should go?," Moses learned self-denial.

Moses had to learn to completely depend on God so that he could lead a completely dependent people. The day he killed the Egyptian for beating a slave he had acted on his own motives with the belief that *he* would deliver the Hebrews. He knew that he would be used by God, but he didn't fully understand that it would only be by the power of God, by the means of God, and by the appointment of God. Forty years later, Moses returned to Egypt from Midian and stood before Pharaoh with a shepherd's rod in his hand, with the full knowledge that *God* would be the one to deliver the Hebrews— the power, the means, and the timing was right.

The life of Moses teaches us that sometimes our experiences in the wilderness are preparing us for something bigger that God has in mind for our lives. If we pray for God to use us to accomplish his will and we trust him completely to bring about his will, in his way, and in his perfect timing, we have to know that he will prepare us for what is coming down the road— sometimes in ways that we don't understand. God uses the wilderness to shape us into the people he wants us to be, and he's given us his Word to help us endure trials and withstand the temptations we are sure to face.

IN HIS STEPS

Jesus lived perfectly under the direction of God's Word. He allowed the words of his Father to lead him and protect him while he was here on Earth. In Matthew 4:1-11, we read how he responded with Scripture to oppose Satan's temptations in the wilderness. In the same way, if we fill our hearts and minds with the Word of God, we will stand ready with the weapon we need to combat the wilderness temptations we are certain to face.

In Psalm 119:133, David made this plea to God:

"_____ my _____ by Your _____, and let no

_____ have _____ over me."

As we are daily walking to the Promised Land, this should be our prayer, too!

Wilderness walking is daily living. It's the hour-to-hour life of the Christian. Our goal each day is to keep stepping in the right direction on the path that will lead us to Heaven. We want, at the end of the day, to be spiritually closer to our destination. We don't want to become wanderers like the Israelites! There will be difficult sections of the road; there will be times that we will have to take a detour; there will be moments when we wonder why we ever left Egypt—our former life of comfortable oppression; but we must not give up and go back! Our Scripture text for this chapter, Psalm 37:3-5, tells us what we need to do to keep walking strong every day:

Trust in the Lord, do good, dwell in the land, and feed on his faithfulness. What does trusting in the Lord look like in normal, everyday living? It's believing that God is always in control. It's understanding that God holds *you* in the palm of his hand, along with yesterday and tomorrow. It's the confident realization that you are a part of something much bigger than the moment in which you are standing right now. So, knowing these things, you keep living, you keep doing good, and you keep enduring because God is faithful; he will not fail you!

Delight in the Lord, and he will give you the desires of your heart. Be happy about the Lord! Love him! Enjoy him! Take care of him! Treat him like he is the most important person in your life! Remember that he is the reason you have hope, and he is the source of your joy; so be kind to him! When you delight in the Lord, he will deliver to you the things which you long for the most. What do you desire? (Think carefully on this). What is it that you *truly* want? It would be more appropriate in the context of this verse to ask, "What does someone *who delights in the Lord* truly want?"

When you give yourself entirely to God—your heart, your mind, your soul—then your desires will fall in line with his, and when that happens, there will be no limit to the outpouring of his blessings in your life. He will shower you with the yearnings of your heart because you have a heart that yearns for him.

Commit your way to the Lord, trust in him, and he will bring it to pass. In the original text, the word "commit" is translated from the Hebrew word *galal,* which literally means "to roll." The word "way" is from the Hebrew word *derek* which refers to "a path, a road, or a journey." This paints such a beautiful picture in my mind, of rolling our path away from ourselves and into the hands of God. It's entrusting him with the very course of our lives. It's giving him our wilderness and placing our journey under his complete care. When we do that with confidence, he will accomplish our hopes, our dreams, and our futures. We can stop stressing, stop worrying, and stop living in fear because there is comfort and reassurance in knowing that God is daily directing our journey. David's son, Solomon, wrote similar words in Proverbs 3:5-6, *"Trust in the Lord with all of your heart, and lean not on your own understanding; in all your ways acknowledge Him, and He shall direct your paths."*

STRENGTH

To become stronger walkers, we have to have God's help. The Bible tells us that our strength comes from him, from his Word, and from times of waiting on him (Psalm 46:1, 119:28, Isaiah 40:31).

> **How do we receive strength from God? How do become stronger through his Word? How can waiting for God's perfect timing make us stronger?**

> **Think again about Psalm 37:3-5. Next to each word below, write down the ways those actions are, or can be, evidenced in your life. (e.g., How do you demonstrate trust in God? In what ways do you show your delight in the Lord? How have you rolled your journey into his hands?)**

> *Trust –*

Delight –

Commit –

TRIALS

Like the wilderness experience of the Israelites, our daily lives are subject to challenges and hardships. Think for a moment about the trials that have been a part of your wilderness over the past weeks, months, and years. How have you endured them? What inspired you to keep on keeping on? What would you tell someone who is standing face to face with a trial you have suffered through?

God doesn't wish pain on his children. He is a good father. When we cry tears of pain, I believe with all of my heart that God cries with us and that he aches to reach down and hold us in his arms. God didn't create suffering—it's never what he wanted for his family, but because it is now a part of our world as a consequence of sin, we can rely on his providence to sustain us.

How does God take care of his people even through the heartbreak that comes with suffering in the wilderness?

How have you seen the providence of God at work in your life?

Encouragement

Read all of Psalm 37. Make a list below of the blessings of the righteous and the afflictions of the wicked. I've written in an example from verses 1-4. Compare the list when you've finished and be encouraged by the ways God takes care of his righteous people!

RIGHTEOUS

given the desires of your heart

WICKED

cut down / wither

Prayer

Heavenly Father, I pray as I begin this study, that my heart will be open to your Word. Direct my steps and keep me from sin.

Help me understand what it means to live daily as a disciple of Christ and to walk with a spiritual purpose. I pray each step I take will bring me closer Home.

I praise you for my redemption and deliverance from sin through Jesus Christ.

Forgive me when I doubt, and forgive me when I am afraid.

Thank you for taking care of me and for showing me glimpses of your glory in the wilderness.

Thank you for being with me as I'm walking to Heaven.

In Jesus' Name, Amen

WALK WITH THE DOC

Walking tip: Walk in the Wilderness

One way to ensure long term adherence to a walking program is to keep it interesting and challenging. That can be achieved by taking an occasional walk in the "wilderness" by choosing to walk on a primitive path that is unfamiliar to you and not well traveled. When confronted with the unknown, no doubt there will be some stress and an accompanied enhancement of the senses. The word "stress" generally has a bad connotation, but not in this instance. Some short-lived stress can be very beneficial. It pushes you to a level of optimal alertness and enhances both behavioral and cognitive performance. You feel more alive. Avoid clinging to the mundane. Experience the challenges that arise from periodically stepping outside of your comfort zone and tackling the road less traveled. It can strengthen the body and sharpen the mind.

TAKE ACTION!

Your challenge is to do something different! If you haven't been involved in any form of exercise, start today! Walking is a great place to begin. If you already exercise regularly, change it up! For example, if you work-out on a treadmill, try taking a walking outside; if you walk in your neighborhood, try a different route. The idea is not to do the same thing every day. Step out of your comfort zone and tackle the road less traveled!

CHAPTER TWO
THE BLESSED LIFE EVER!
Walk in the Ways of the Lord

"You shall walk in all the ways which the Lord your God has commanded you, that you may live and that it may be well with you, and that you may prolong your days in the land which you shall possess" (Deuteronomy 5:33).

They say that the way you walk can tell people a lot about who you are. Results from studies conducted over the years reveal that the characteristics of a person's natural gait can be reflective of emotions, mood, and even personality. For example, people who walk with their weight shifted slightly forward and take quick steps (probably checking items off their to-do lists as they go) are typically intelligent, confident, and like to "get things done." People who walk with their chest lifted, head up, shoulders back, and have a bit of a bounce to their steps are generally fun, enthusiastic, and get along well with others. The findings of those studies aren't always accurate, but it's interesting to see the trends. It also makes me think about the way *I* walk and what people might assume about *me* as I'm stepping through the day.

When I think of differences in walking styles, I can't help but think about my husband and my dad. They are different in the way they walk, and consistent with the findings of the study, their personalities are different, too. My dad walks fast, like he's on a mission. If he's on a trail, he uses walking poles, and he's most likely meditating, praying, or reviewing the periodic table of elements to the rhythm of his steps. Sam, on the other hand, will tell you that his walk is more of a "lumber." He's not really worried about pace, and his form will probably not make you think of a gazelle. But, they both like being out in nature, and they both like spending time with people they love—two things they both can enjoy while walking.

One time, Dad and Sam decided to go on a hike together, just the two of them, for some Father-Son-in-Law bonding. As they started off, Dad took the lead and Sam was right behind him. After awhile my dad looked back and Sam was nowhere to be seen! He waited until Sam finally appeared on the trail in the distance—*huffing and puffing!* Sam talks about how after a few steps into the hike, he had looked up and Dad was just a tiny dot; and my dad still jokes today about how he had been pouring out his heart and soul to "only the trees" for almost a mile! They worked it out, each of them making some adjustments in their walk, and they reached the end of the trail together.

Just as your physical walk can tell others something about who you are, the same is true with your spiritual walk. People watch the spiritual steps you take and draw conclusions about the things that bring you joy and the things that you love. In fact, your spiritual walk can reveal what is most important to you and the direction you're headed. Because of this, it's important to be mindful of *the way* we're walking spiritually, as well as *why* we're walking, and *where* we're walking.

There are a number of verses in the Bible that tell God's people to *walk in the way of the Lord.* What is the way of the Lord? How are we supposed to know if we're walking in his way? What should be our motivation for walking there? Let's take a look...

God's Way

The words found in Deuteronomy 5:33 (and written at the beginning of this chapter) were spoken by Moses as he reviewed God's commandments with the children of Israel just before they crossed into the Land of Promise. He wanted them to be reminded of all the laws that God had given and to remember that they were to *walk* in them! Remember that *walking,* in the Scriptures that are a part of this study, refers to *the manner in which we live.* So, in these verses we find the Israelites being told to live their lives in the ways that they had been instructed by God.

In his prayer to God for the dedication of the temple, King Solomon said, *"... then hear in Heaven, and forgive the sin of Your servants, Your people Israel, that You may teach them the good way in which they should walk; and send rain on Your land which You have given to Your people as an inheritance."* By reading this verse found in 1 Kings 8:36, we can know that the ways in which the Israelites were to walk were good and, once again, that they were taught by God.

What were those "ways"?

David, a man whose heart longed to know God, often meditated on the ways of the Lord. He wrote about his sincere desire to learn and walk in those ways in the 119th Psalm. In the first 40 verses of the psalm David identifies the Lord's "ways" as the following:

- His laws
- His precepts
- His testimonies
- His statutes
- His commandments
- His word
- His judgments

This psalm of David's, and many of his others, helps us understand that the ways of the Lord are those things that God has told us to do. God's ways are his rules, his expectations, and his desires for his people. The Israelites learned the ways of God through Moses. God spoke his commands to Moses and then Moses told them to the people. Today we learn God's ways as he speaks to us through the Bible, which is his Word. By the pens of inspired men, he has taught us his ways and they are good, just as Solomon said.

To walk in the ways of the Lord is to live according to God's Word. Plain and simple. Or at least, the idea is easy enough. Doing it...*living it*...can be challenging at times. Not because God has made it difficult, but because we're human and live in a world that is characterized by sin. Walking in step with the world around us might be comfortable and convenient, but it's a course that results in wilderness wandering; it's a journey without direction and one that will ultimately end in a desert death. That's not what God wants for you...or me...or *anyone*. He is crying out to all people every-where, "Follow Me...I have a better way!"

In his way there is joy. In his way there is blessing. In his way there is hope. Because his way leads to Heaven.

Blessings Follow

Look again at Deuteronomy 5:33, and notice the reasons Moses gave the Israelites for walking in ways God had commanded:

- That you may live
- That it may be well with you
- That you may prolong your days

If they walked in the ways God had commanded, their lives would be blessed! Not with just a small, quickly forgotten blessing—but the blessing of life...a *good* life...a *long and good* life!

In another of the psalms, David begins by saying, *"Blessed is every one who fears the Lord, who walks in His ways"* (Psalm 128:1). The word *blessed* means "happy" in this context. People who fear the Lord and follow his commandments are happy! And this doesn't apply to just a few, but rather, to *everyone.* If our spiritual walk is characterized by reverence and obedience, we will be blessed!

When the Israelites were in the wilderness they had the experience of present-blessing along with the promise of future-blessing. The wilderness had its difficulties, but as long as they trusted God and obeyed him, he would take care of them. He would shower them with desert blessings: food, water, good health, and victory over their enemies; and they could enjoy those blessings while living under the umbrella-promise of Canaan.

The same is true for us today. If we fear God, we will obey him; and when we obey God, the blessings will come—in the present *and* in the future.

We Are All Winners

One Sunday morning, in Kate's Bible class, the teacher began to explain the rules of a trivia game they were going to play. She told the kids that they really needed to listen carefully because if they didn't hear the question, then they might not get the answer correct and their team could end up losing the game. With that, my daughter promptly shot her hand up in the air. The teacher called on her, "Yes, Kate?"

And with all the passion her four-year-old self could muster, Kate announced: "MY mom says that we are ALL winners."

Now, I am sure that those words have come out of my mouth countless times. I know that I've said, "We are all winners" when my kids try to make everything a race, or when they try to "rub in" a win, or when they really tried their best but didn't get first place. However, I'm all about friendly competition! Luckily her teacher was a good friend of mine. Otherwise I might have been embarrassed. *Oh, Kate has one of those moms.* My friend just laughed and said, "Well, that's true, Kate. We are all winners, but let's see who can get the most points!"

A wonderful thing about being a Christian is knowing that you've already won. One of the first things I do when I get a new Bible is turn to the book of Revelation and right above the title I write the words, "WE WIN!" Because we do! We know the ending! The devil loses and God wins. The devil will be cast into the lake of fire, and God will save his family. If we walk in the ways of the Lord, we will have eternal life in Heaven. This is our greatest blessing! If you are in Christ (Galatians 3:27), and you live faithfully according to God's Word (Revelation 2:10), then you are a winner. God has made you that promise (1 John 2:25).

A WALKING WARRIOR

There are many examples in the Bible of men and women who walked in the ways of the Lord. These are people who loved God and had a sincere desire to follow his commands. Their actions were characterized by faith and obedience as they lived their lives. They're the ones we cheer for through their stories as they come up against evil and face disaster. Sometimes they frustrate us with their choices, but they never let us down, because even when they get lost in the darkness of sin for a spell, they always find God's way again.

When I think about someone in Scripture who walked in the ways of the Lord, the picture of a shepherd boy turned chosen king comes to my mind: David, who God called *"a man after His own heart."*

How did David come to be seen in God's eyes as a man with a heart like His? The answer can be found in scene after scene throughout the reel of David's life, and despite his imperfections (and flat-out failures), his life in motion is a testimony to immeasurable faith. In the familiar story of David and the Philistine warrior, Goliath, we discover that David reflected the heart of God because he had relinquished his heart to God.

The Israelite army stood on one mountain and the army of the Philistines stood on another. They faced each other in preparation for battle with the Valley of Elah stretched between them. The champion of the Philistines, Goliath, a giant of a man, challenged the Israelites to send someone to fight him. If he were to be killed, his people would become the servants of the Israelites, but if he were to kill his opponent, then the Israelites would become servants of the Philistines. All of Israel, along with their king, was discouraged and frightened. For forty days, Goliath cried out, "I defy the armies of Israel this day; give me a man, that we may fight together!"

David had been sent by his father, Jesse, to check on his brothers and to take them food, as they camped out with the Israelite army. When he reached the battlefront and saw Goliath, heard his threats, and witnessed the fear of the people, in frustration he asked, "Who is this uncircumcised Philistine that he should defy the armies of the living God?" David stood in front of King Saul and said, "I will go and fight this Philistine…the Lord will deliver me!"

He didn't wear armor, he didn't carry a sword, and he didn't hold a shield; David faced Goliath with only a sling, five stones, and his faith. If we could have looked into his shepherd's bag and each of those five stones had represented one aspect of David's character, I believe this is what we would have found:

- One stone of obedience
- One stone of devotion
- One stone of trust
- One stone of repentance
- One stone of steadfast love

The stones in David's bag

David didn't live a perfect life, but the virtuous stones in his bag tell the story of a man who dedicated his life to walking in the ways of the Lord.

DAVID OBEYED GOD WILLINGLY AND REVERENTLY. In 1 Samuel 13:14, Samuel confronted Saul about his unlawful sacrifice. He said, *"But now your kingdom shall not continue. The Lord has sought for himself a man after His own heart, and the Lord has commanded him to be commander over His people, because you have not kept what the Lord commanded you."*

We also read in Acts 13:22, the words of Paul as he spoke at the synagogue in Antioch, *"...He raised up for them David as king, to whom also He gave testimony and said, 'I have found David the son of Jesse, a man after My own heart, who will do all My will."*

We learn from these verses that David had a heart like God's because he was obedient to the will of God. When God told him to do something, he did it…and he did it with joy. When you read the psalms he wrote, you can see the love he had for God and for God's laws. He understood that the ways of God were much better than his own, and he praised God again and again for His righteous, faithful, and perfect Word.

DAVID DEVOTED HIMSELF TO WORSHIPING AND SERVING GOD. In 1 Kings 11:4, we read what happened as a result of Solomon having many wives and concubines: *"For it was so, when Solomon was old, that his wives turned his heart after other gods; and his heart was not loyal to the Lord his God, as was the heart of his father David."*

There was loyalty in David's heart. He served God all the days of his life—from his days as a shepherd, to his days in exile, to his days as the ruler of the Israelite kingdom. He looked to God for guidance before making decisions and credited God for his successes. His worship through song and poetry was so pure and beautiful that the psalms he wrote thousands of years ago continue to lead the hearts and minds of Christians in praise and prayer today.

DAVID TRUSTED GOD COMPLETELY AND CONTINUALLY. Read these words of David, found in 1 Samuel 17:45-47, as he prepared to fight Goliath: *"You come to me with a sword, with a spear, and with a javelin. But I come to you in the name of the Lord of hosts, the God of the armies of Israel, whom you have defied. This day the Lord will deliver you into my hand, and I will strike you and take your head from you. And this day I will give the carcasses of the camp of the Philistines to the birds of the air and the wild beasts of the earth, that all the earth may know that there is a God in Israel. Then all this* *assembly shall know that the Lord does not save with sword and spear; for the battle is the Lord's and He will give you into our hands."*

The raw trust in David's words! The power in his stand! It gives me the chills when I read it. If you read on through verse 48, there is something even more incredible. David ran toward the Philistine army to meet Goliath. He *ran*. He looked directly in the eyes of a bloodthirsty giant, and he ran toward him with no sword, no shield, and no armor. His chance of winning rested only in the hands of God. So he ran. He ran with complete trust in God to deliver him and save his nation. I pray that when I face enemy giants in my life I can run toward them with unwavering confidence in knowing that God will protect me, just as David did.

DAVID REPENTED OF HIS SINS SINCERELY AND WITH DEEP SORROW.

"Have mercy upon me, O God, according to Your loving-kindness; according to the multitude of Your tender mercies, blot out my transgressions. Wash me thoroughly from my iniquity, and cleanse me from my sin." These words begin the 51st psalm, written by David as his heart was heavy with sadness and guilt over the sin he had committed with Bathsheba.

David was not a perfect man, but he was a faithful man. He always found God's way again. Satan likes to use our guilt to keep us away from God. When we've done something wrong, he likes to make us think that we're not worthy to be a child of God or that we can't possibly be forgiven. Because David had a heart like God's, he knew that God would always love him and would always forgive him, and David always came back. He may not have always felt forgiven, but he acted forgiven. The faithful life he lived, marked by sin but restored through repentance, is an inspiration to imperfect people who want to have a close relationship with God.

DAVID LOVED GOD STEADFASTLY AND WITHOUT RESTRAINT. I think

this is the stone that brought Goliath to the ground. Love conquers! It was because of his love for God that he would not tolerate an enemy tearing down His people. It was because of his love for God that he lived an obedient, devoted, loyal, and repentant life. He loved God, so he gave his heart to him, and God shaped it into a heart like his own.

"I will love You, O Lord, my strength. The Lord is my rock and my fortress and my deliverer; My God, my strength, in whom I will trust; my shield and the horn of my salvation, my stronghold. I will call upon the Lord, who is worthy

to be praised; so shall I be saved from my enemies" (Psalm 18:1-3).

David loved God, walked in his ways, and was wonderfully blessed. From his lineage would come a man in many ways like himself—even called the Son of David. A man also born in Bethlehem, a Shepherd, an exiled King, sent by his Father, rejected by his brothers, and who would defeat the greatest enemy the world had ever seen. This would be no ordinary man! This would be the Messiah, the Savior of mankind, the Son of the Almighty God who would conquer the giant of sin and death and reign eternally on a throne in Heaven!

IN HIS STEPS

Everything that Jesus did while he lived on this earth was in obedience to God. Read John 6:38 and fill in the blanks:

"For I have come down from Heaven, not to do _____ _____ _____, but the _____ of _____ who sent Me."

OUR DAILY WALK _____

To walk in the ways of the Lord we have to begin every day with a recommitment to obey him. Before we move our feet from the bed to the floor we have to make the decision that the entire day will be lived for God. It is a conscious choice. Pray these words, "Today I will walk in the ways you have commanded. Today, I will live for YOU. Today, I will follow your direction and trust your guidance."

It may seem unnecessary to say those words that seem to be so obvious, so full of common sense, but remember that our daily spiritual walk must be intentional. We should remind ourselves at the beginning of every day's journey that our walk will be in harmony with God's ways.

Can you imagine how this might have helped the Israelites in the wilderness? If they each had started every day with a personal pledge to walk in the ways of the Lord, there might have been less grumbling and more encouraging, less doubting and more trusting, less golden calf building and more worshiping of the true God who saved them from bondage.

Here is the catch when it comes to walking in the ways of the Lord....you have to *KNOW* his ways. Your life cannot be lived in obedience to God when you don't know what he expects from you. We can read his Word and know with confidence what he has commanded. We can also know the benefits that come with obedience as well as the consequences that result from disobedience. It is important to spend time every day in Bible study. Through personal devotion to God's Word we come to know and understand his ways. Then, we commit to living our lives according to those ways.

As you walk through each day, remember that obedience in the "small" things is as important as obedience in the "big" things. When we are mindful, moment to moment, of our thoughts, our words, and our actions, we are building a bridge of virtue, plank-by-plank; so that when difficult choices come or tempting situations arise, we already have a sturdy support in which to safely cross over the pitfall of sin.

STRENGTH

We can find strength in knowing that the Christian life is the better life. It's not a life of ease, but it is a life of blessing. In fact, we're told in the Bible that it's a life that is characterized by rejection, suffering, and persecution. What makes it a better life is the promise of Heaven. It's the promise that in the end, God's way leads Home.

How do we become stronger when we walk in the ways of the Lord?

What blessings have you experienced in this life because you are a Christian?

What confidence can we have in a life of faithful obedience to God?

TRIALS

Walking in the ways of the Lord is not always the popular thing to do in the world today. More and more often taking a stand for the Truth is going to mean taking a stand against mainstream society and facing consequences for being a Christian. We need to remember that this is not a new reality. We are walking in the steps of many faithful brothers and sisters who have gone before us; as they fought they good fight, so must we!

What challenges do we face when we commit to walking in the ways of the Lord?

How do we overcome those challenges?

ENCOURAGEMENT

Take some time to read all of Psalm 119. This psalm was written in the form of an alphabetic acrostic. The chapter is divided into 22 stanzas each representing a letter from the Hebrew alphabet and the eight lines within each stanza begin with that letter. If this psalm had been written in the English language, the eight lines of the first stanza would begin with "A," the eight lines of the second stanza would begin with "B," and so on through the end of the alphabet.

I challenge you to write an acrostic psalm using the letters of your first name! (If your name is really long, you can just use your initials). Write about your love for God's Word and try to create at least two lines per stanza.

Here is an example for you:

Lord, you have given me hope
Let it strengthen and keep me
On days that are dark
On nights that seem endless
Raise my spirit
Revive the fire in my heart
Inspire me with your promises
In your way I will find my way Home

This can be a precious gift of encouragement to a friend, too. Using the letters of your friend's name, write an acrostic poem telling her why she's special and what she means to you. Or do this for your spouse—it's a wonderful way to express your feelings in a simple and unique way.

PRAYER

Father in Heaven, thank you for teaching me your ways. I pray that I will faithfully walk in them as I live day to day. I humbly ask for a heart like yours.

Help me to trust in your direction and to obey your Word. Forgive me when I try to lean on my own understanding. Give me the wisdom to stay on your path and the strength to get back on when I fall to the side.

I pray for courage in times of trial and confidence to stand on the Truth. Help me to be mindful of the example I am setting for the people around me.

Thank you for your blessings—the blessings I enjoy every single day, and the blessings to come when I reach my Heavenly Home.

In Jesus' Name, Amen

WALK WITH THE DOC

Walking Tip: Walk for longevity

Do you want to add years to your life and life to your years?
While it is true that aging is inevitable and death is certain,
through lifestyle management we can make the most of the time
we are allotted here on Earth. Genetics defines our risk, but how
we chose to manage that risk through lifestyle choice is far more
important. How we opt to live our lives determines ultimately
the nature and time of our death. Life expectancy in the United
States is just under 80 years, and yet we are 43rd in the world in
that regard. One thing we can do better is to be less sedentary.
Walkers live longer and fast walkers live longer still. Walking the
road toward wellness will add quality to your life and precious
additional years.

TAKE ACTION!

Have you considered the benefits of walking? In the appendix
I've included a list of 100 reasons to exercise. Pick the ten that
you feel would be the greatest benefit to you personally and
focus on those as you begin a walking program. You might
consider writing your top ten reasons down on a piece of paper
or index card and then putting them somewhere you will see
them regularly. They will serve as helpful reminders of why you
should keep "walking the road to wellness."

CHAPTER THREE
FLAWLESS FOOTSTEPS
Walk as Christ Walked

"He who says he abides in Him ought himself also to walk just as He walked" (1 John 2:6).

I remember taking the picture. Briggs had just figured out how the whole door knob thing works, and on this particular afternoon, he kept opening the door in the kitchen that leads into our garage. This is a door that we didn't want Briggs to open because just on the other side there are three steps that lead to a concrete floor. So, Sam stood behind Briggs, and when Briggs would open the door, Sam would shut it again and give Briggs a firm "No."

After a few rounds of opening and shutting, Sam leaned against the door with one hand, put his other hand on his hip, and crossed his legs. Then Briggs did one of the sweetest things I've ever seen. He tried to copy Sam's exact position…hand on door, crossed legs, and he would have put his hand on his hip too, had it not been for the firm grip on his Sippy cup. That's when I grabbed my camera! In the picture you can see him looking at Sam's legs, just to be sure he has it right. I tell you, it still warms this mom's heart to the very core.

The imitating continued from that day forward. Briggs would watch closely, try as hard as he could to copy Sam's movements perfectly, and then proudly announce, "Look Mommy! Just like Daddy do's!" Today, Briggs still loves to imitate his dad. He wants to be just like him. I love that he wants to be like his dad because I know that his dad wants to be like Christ.

In 1 Corinthians 11:1, Paul wrote these words to the Christians in Corinth, *"Imitate me, just as I also imitate Christ."* Some Bible versions use the word "follow" rather than "imitate," but the original Greek word *mimetes* carries with it the idea of copying or mimicking, so "imitate" would be a more accurate translation. Many people consider themselves to be *followers* of Christ, but I wonder how many of those truly strive to *imitate* him?

Imitating Christ involves trying to pattern my life after his life. It comes from a sincere desire to copy his behavior, his language, his attitude…his *walk*. It's not simply doing what he says, it's making the humble effort to BE LIKE him. In order to be like him, I have to know him. I have to be close to him. I have to carefully place my steps in the footprints he has left throughout the pages of the Bible, and to do that, I need to study the Word, and I need to pray for God's help.

As a Christian, I should try to copy the life of Christ. I have to ask myself every day: am I living in such a way that if someone copies what I do, or if my children imitate my behavior, are they also copying, or imitating, Christ? I won't be able to do it perfectly, of course; I'll be a little off balance…I won't be able to get my foot just right…I may not always be able to let go of the sippy cup…but I will faithfully try.

To walk as Christ walked in our daily lives, we have to take a close look at how he lived his life while he was here on this earth. What was most important to him? What was his purpose? How did he spend his time?

Jesus in the World

I have often wondered what it might have been like to have known Jesus while he was on this earth. I have thought about his relationship with his disciples, with his parents, with the people who hated him, and with his Father in Heaven. I have tried to imagine what he might have looked like or how his voice may have sounded. I have thought about what it would have been like to eat with him or take a walk with him. I have wondered what it would have been like to worship next to him or to hear him teach. I wish I could have just a glimpse of Jesus in everyday life, a glimpse of someone living perfectly and in complete harmony with God's will.

Here is what I do know: Jesus radiated love, and he gave it, liberally. It was his nature. And here is something else that I know: his life—his purpose— was about saving people.

In my mind, I can see the hard-working hands of Jesus gently holding the face of a child, and I can hear him speaking words of reparation to the physically and spiritually broken. I see him touching the eyes of the blind, saving the life of an adulteress woman, talking to God in prayer in the early hours of the morning, and washing the dirt covered feet of Peter. I see him talking to a woman rejected by society, cooking fish on the shore for his disciples, and crying over the death of his dear friend. Everything he did was out of love for God and love for people.

I try to imagine Jesus living in the world today. How would he spend his time? Where would he work? Where would he go to be alone? What would he eat? What would he wear? For me, it can be hard to picture Jesus in this place that is so different from Galilee in 30 A.D., but knowing that he is the same yesterday, today, and forever (Hebrews 13:8), there are some things I can clearly see:

I see him extending forgiveness. I see him offering sinners a better life. I see him teaching people about Heaven and telling them how they can get there. I see him encouraging. I see him worshiping. I see him concerned with suffering, hunger, and homelessness. I see him reaching out to those who are hurting. I see him living his life in humble obedience to God just as the Bible describes he did when he was here over 2000 years ago.

Oh, I want to be like him! I want to reflect that kind of love in my life! I want to draw people to me—*all* people—and I want to extend to them the same love and mercy he has extended to me! I want to show others the joy that comes with doing the will of God! I want to be a living example of faith and share the message that he shared: *God loves you and wants you to love him too! There's a beautiful place called Heaven where there are mansions to spare, and God wants you to be there! Come into the kingdom, the body of Christ, the Church…where there is hope, there is help, and there is healing!*

My prayer is to walk more like him every day.

A WALKING WARRIOR

Walking as Christ walked means stepping out in faith to follow him and to live like him. It's a process—not something that happens overnight. You don't go to sleep one night a struggling sinner and wake up the next morning a faultless follower. Walking as Christ walked is characterized by daily discipleship. It's looking at the virtues of Jesus and making those virtues your own.

I think about Peter. Bless his heart, he struggled in his spiritual walk. But that's one reason I love him and chose him as an example of a "walking warrior." He walked well, then fell; he walked well, then fell; and we witness that pattern in his life through the Scriptures over and over again. We see him boldly step out in faith in one instance, and then in the very next moment, we see him tumble to the ground in doubt or fear. The especially encouraging thing about Peter is that when we look back at the entire landscape of his life, and take our focus off a flower here and a thorn there, we see a follower of Christ who never quit. We see a disciple whose belief blossomed from a tiny seed of hope into a great forest of faith.

The story of Peter walking on the water is one that many of us have heard since our childhood. We can find the account in Matthew 14:22-33. Jesus had just fed over 5000 people after teaching them and healing their sick. When he had sent the crowds away, he told Peter and the other disciples to meet him on the other side of the sea. Jesus wanted to spend time alone on the mountain, in prayer with his Father.

The disciples were far away from the land when the wind became strong, and the waves began to toss their boat back and forth. During the fourth watch, between 3:00 and 6:00 in the morning, Jesus came walking toward them on the water. I find it comforting to know that Jesus was mindful of their situation—he wasn't right there with them, but he knew what they were facing, and he knew how they were feeling. When the men first saw him they thought he was a ghost and were terrified; but Jesus said to them, *"Be of good cheer! It is I; do not be afraid."*

Peter answered, *"Lord, if it is You, command me to come to You on the water."* And Jesus said, *"Come."*

Notice the chain of events and the wonderful lessons wrapped around each link...

He stepped onto the water. Peter left the boat! In the storm and in the dark, Peter left the boat to walk to Jesus. Stepping out of the boat took courage and it tells us something about Peter. He was bold! He had a heart that completely wanted to follow Jesus, and he did things that others didn't have the nerve to do. Peter asked Jesus to give him the command to walk out onto the water, and Jesus gave it. There's a wonderful lesson tucked into Peter's request: sometimes God is just waiting on us to ask! He can do unbelievable and amazing things in our lives; but have we asked him?

HE WALKED OUT IN FAITH. Peter believed Jesus could help him walk on the water. That's why he left the boat! His faith was not weak; in fact, it was stronger than the faith of any other man on the boat that night. I love his passion! I love his spirit! Peter wanted to be more and do more. I imagine he would have been like the kid in class who wiggles around in his seat waving his hand shouting, "Pick me! Pick me!" when he's pretty sure he knows the answer to the teacher's question. He may be wrong, but he's the first to try! With the darkness surrounding him, the wind blowing fiercely, the waves crashing all around, Peter had the faith to walk toward Jesus.

HE SANK DOWN IN FEAR. Peter took his eyes off Jesus long enough to see the terrible storm around him, and he became afraid. He began to sink when he let his fear overcome his faith. He cried out to Jesus, *"Lord, save me!"* and Jesus caught him. Peter didn't doubt that Jesus could help him walk on top of the water, and he didn't doubt that Jesus could save him in the end; but somewhere in between he took his eyes off of Jesus and doubted that Jesus was stronger than the storm. When I read James 1:6, I can't help but see this picture of Peter sinking into the sea. James was writing about believing in God's ability to answer our prayers and said, *"But let him ask in faith, with no doubting, for he who doubts is like a wave of the sea driven and tossed by the wind."*

HE LIVED THROUGH A TEST. Jesus saved Peter and helped him get back to the boat. Did he hold Peter's hand? Did he carry Peter? The Bible doesn't say, but I believe that Jesus' words, *"O you of little faith, why did you doubt?"* must have landed hard in Peter's heart and echoed in his mind over and over as they made their way back to the boat. The wind stopped. The test was over. How did Peter do? Some might say he failed; he doubted Jesus and sank. But I disagree! Peter's faith grew that morning as well as the faith of every man on that boat (Matthew 14:33)! Peter had seen Jesus perform miracles before; and now he could see that Jesus could accomplish the miraculous through him as well. This was a tremendous lesson for Peter! He also learned the importance of staying focused on Jesus despite the storms raging all around him, and that the hand of Jesus would always be close and ready to save. Peter lived through a test and became stronger for it! These lessons would serve him well after Jesus returned to Heaven, leaving Peter with the most important set of keys known to man (Matthew 16:13-20).

HE BECAME MORE LIKE CHRIST. Peter had a desire to walk as Christ walked. He didn't do it perfectly, but we can look at his life and see how his steps fell closer and closer in line with the steps of Christ as he matured in his faith. The Peter who sank in the water just a few feet away from Jesus is the same Peter who wrote these words:

"Blessed be the God and Father of our Lord Jesus Christ, who according to His abundant mercy has begotten us again to a living hope through the resurrection of Jesus Christ from the dead, to an inheritance incorruptible and undefiled and that does not fade away, reserved in heaven for you, who are kept by the power of God through faith for salvation ready to be revealed in the last time. In this you greatly rejoice, though now for a little while, if need be, you have been grieved by various trials, that the genuineness of your faith, being much more precious than gold that perishes, though it is tested by fire, may be found to praise, honor, and glory at the revelation of Jesus Christ, whom having not seen you love. Though now you do not see Him, yet believing, you rejoice with joy inexpressible and full of glory, receiving the end of your faith— the salvation of your souls" (1 Peter 1:3-8).

One time I heard a preacher say that between the Gospels and the book of Acts, the Disciples changed from "Christ with us" to "Christ in us." I love that. Peter went from physically walking through cities all over Judea by Jesus' side to spiritually walking in the footsteps of his risen Savior. One test at a time, one lesson at a time, one step at a time, Peter became more like Christ.

IN HIS STEPS

We are to walk as Jesus walked and sometimes that walk is characterized by grief and wrongful suffering...even when we do good. Endure, friend, and God will be pleased. Read what Peter wrote in 1 Peter 2:21 and fill in the blanks:

"For to this you were called, because _____ also suffered for us, leaving us an _____, that you should _____ His _____."

When I think about how we should live every day with the goal of walking as Christ walked, I'm reminded of this story that has been told about General Robert E. Lee:

Prior to the unpleasantness of 1861, while Lee's children were still young, he went out early one morning for a walk. A gentle snow had fallen the night before, and there was a beautiful blanket of snow covering the path. As he walked along, he could hear the faint sound of small footsteps behind him. Lee looked back and found that his little boy Custis was behind him, imitating his every move and walking in the very tracks his father had made in the snow. Step for step the boy was struggling to ensure that each of his steps fell in the exact footprint left by his father.

"When I saw this," Lee told one of his friends long afterwards, "I said to myself, 'it behooves me to walk very straight when this fellow is already following in my tracks'" (http://www.old-picture.com/defining-moments/Footsteps-Father.htm).

People are watching you: younger people, older people, people you may not even realize are watching. They're taking notice of where you walk and how you walk. They may be walking right behind you and trying to place their feet exactly in the marks your steps have made on the path. Your journey matters—not only because of where it is taking *you*, but also because of where it's taking the people who are following your footsteps. If you are walking like Christ, you will be walking straight, and you'll be walking Home.

In the words of Jesus, the life of a Christian involves daily cross-carrying and following after him (Luke 9:43). It's a life that is characterized by self-denial and learning to ask ourselves the question, "What would Jesus do?" instead of, "What do *I* want to do?" Since the mid-90s WWJD bracelet craze, the question "What would Jesus do?" has become somewhat cliché, which is sad, because in its rawest sense, this simple yet profound thought, should encapsulate the life of a Christ follower.

Every single day, our sincere desire should be to live like Christ. If we are living like him, then his light will shine through our lives and be seen by the people around us. I want his light to be reflected in everything that I do, from how I treat my husband, to how I raise my children, to how I extend kindness to others. I want it to be reflected in every decision I make, from the little ones to the life-changing ones. I want it to be reflected through how I demonstrate compassion, good works, wisdom, and (most importantly) how I show love. I will not do this perfectly. In fact, I know I will fail. But then I'll think of Peter, and with my eyes on Jesus, I'll step out onto the water.

Strength

As Christians, we are the aroma of Christ, we are Christ in the world, and we are his representation on this earth. When we walk as Christ walked, we will change lives, not because of our own ability or effort, but because our footsteps will lead others closer to God.

How do we come to know Jesus better so that we can imitate him in our everyday lives?

How will we become better and stronger travelers by walking as Jesus walked?

Trials

Christ suffered. We have to know that if we are walking in his footsteps, we will suffer too.

Sometimes, in certain situations, asking the question "What would Jesus do?" will give us an answer that requires sacrifice—it might mean "denying yourself and taking up your cross" (Matthew 16:24).

What does that mean? How do we deny ourselves and in what ways do we "carry our cross?"

How do we get through those times of self-denial and keep on walking?

We're not perfect, and that's okay! Sometimes we forget that wilderness walking is not always easy, and we can be really hard on ourselves. There is comfort in knowing that Jesus understands. Think about that for a minute. Not superficially, not casually; but he sincerely and empathetically understands every twist and turn of our wilderness walk. And he is on our side. He is advocating for us; pleading on our behalf. Keep following him and imitating him!

Read Hebrews 2:18, Hebrews 4:15, and 1 John 2:1. What do you learn from these verses?

ENCOURAGEMENT

In the beautiful sermon Jesus preached from the mountain at the beginning of his ministry, he talked about how to live a life that is pleasing to God. He revealed to the crowd, and to his followers throughout time, important principles of discipleship that should be a part of who we are and how we live.

I am going to challenge you to do something that will affect you and your prayer life profoundly. When you enter into your personal time of prayer with God, open up your Bible to Matthew 5. Place your Bible in your lap, or set it on the floor, on the bed, or on the table in front of you. Begin by silently reading verses 3-12. When you have finished reading them, go back and pray out loud for God to help you demonstrate each of the beatitudes in your own life.

For example: "Help me to be poor in spirit. Help me when I mourn. Help me to be meek. Help me to hunger and thirst for righteousness. Help me to be merciful. Help me to be pure in heart. Help me to be a peacemaker. Help me when I am persecuted for the sake of righteousness."

The next time you pray, focus on another aspect of the Sermon on the Mount (Matthew 5-7). Read the words of Christ, and then pray for his teachings to take root in your heart and to be revealed in your life.

Help me to love my enemies. Help me to build my house on the rock. Help me not to worry. Help me not to be hypocritical. And on and on.

This is life-changing! As we walk like Christ, we become more Christ-like.

PRAYER

Father, thank you for Jesus. Thank you for sending him to this earth to live and to die so that I can have hope. Thank you for providing me a way to have my sins taken away so I can be with you in Heaven eternally.

I pray that you help me walk in the footsteps of Jesus. Help me to learn his example and then to live his example so that I can show others what it means to be a follower of Christ.

Give me strength to bear my cross each day.

Give me a heart of compassion and a love like yours.

In Jesus' Name, Amen

WALK WITH THE DOC

Walking tip: Walk purposefully

Plan your walk and walk your plan. Allocating the time seems to be a major roadblock for many. It is important to understand and embrace the many reasons why walking reaps so many rewards. Knowing what those rewards are and understanding the science behind them will be a constant reminder that time walking is time well spent. Walking is a simple, inexpensive, readily accessible way to improve health and fitness, and it is available at no cost. Those countries that have longer life expectancies enjoy walking as their primary form of exercise. Be deliberate in carrying out your goal oriented walking program. Mix it up. Walk different venues: trails, parks, greenways, etc. Keep it interesting. Spread the word......walk, walk, walk.

TAKE ACTION!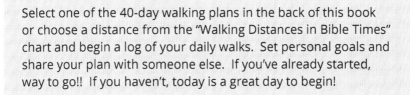

Select one of the 40-day walking plans in the back of this book or choose a distance from the "Walking Distances in Bible Times" chart and begin a log of your daily walks. Set personal goals and share your plan with someone else. If you've already started, way to go!! If you haven't, today is a great day to begin!

CHAPTER FOUR
THE VIEW FROM DOWN HERE
Walk Humbly

"He has shown you, O man, what is good; and what does the Lord require of you but to do justly, to love mercy, and to walk humbly with your God?" (Micah 6:8).

I entered into the profession of nursing with a lofty vision. I chose this field because of my deep love for people and the sincere desire I have to make a difference in the lives of others. While completing my undergraduate work, and then through the long semesters of nursing school, I imagined the day when I would be finished with all of my schooling and could spend my time just making everybody feel better. (I had quite a lofty vision).

After graduating from nursing school and landing my first job in a hospital, it didn't take long for me to find that nursing is not always about making people feel better; there is a side to nursing that is heartbreaking and sometimes even cruel. A band aid doesn't always stop the pain, and sometimes the "bad guy" wins despite the most heroic of efforts. This was a hard lesson for a 22-year-old girl with a crisp set of hot pink scrubs, a brand new Littmann stethoscope, and a dog-eared drug handbook, who came out of nursing school ready to fix the world.

While working in a Cardiac Intensive Care Unit, with two years of experience under my drawstring, I had grown accustomed to physically and emotionally draining shifts. Many times I spent my drive home in tears, sometimes happy and sometimes sad, and often wondered why I chose such a demanding career. Then the shift came that forever changed my perspective.

One of my patients had been battling cardiogenic shock after suffering a massive heart attack and had spent days on the ventilator with a collection of life-sustaining IV medications. She was very sick. I had spent all day working with her: titrating her infusions, suctioning her endotracheal tube, measuring her cardiac output, monitoring her temperature, and repositioning her for comfort. I was constantly conversing with the physicians and providing support to her loved ones. It had become clear that despite our best efforts her condition was not improving, and the difficult decision was made to end her treatment. She died peacefully surrounded by her family.

At the end of my shift, after completing my paperwork, making all the necessary phone calls, and saying goodbye to the last family member, I sat down and the tears came before I could make it to the car. I literally sobbed. As I sat in the nurses' station with my face in my hands, I felt a hand on my shoulder. To this day I have no idea who she was, but I looked up into the face of an older nurse.

"Please tell me this gets easier," I said.

"Nope," she answered, *"it doesn't, and if it ever does, then it'll be time for you to start doing something else for a living."*

That was it. She walked away, leaving me alone with my perspective changing moment: the sudden realization that nursing is complex, contradictory, a blessing, and a challenge all rolled into one extraordinary profession made for the strong willed but tender hearted.

I've learned that nursing is not always about "fixing" people but more about helping people through their unique journeys—regardless of their destinations. It's about offering hope and comfort to people, whatever road they may be on. It's supporting others, caring for others, and serving others in their times of need. True nursing is achieved when I stop thinking about what I get out of my profession and begin focusing on what I give. My lofty vision is now humble and gratified.

Having a vision in our jobs is important because it keeps us focused on why we do what we do, it prepares us for challenges, and it motivates us to perform well. When it comes to our Christianity, having a vision is not just important; it's necessary. It's necessary because it's a vision that extends past the boundary of earthly life and influences the eternal.

What is my vision when it comes to Christianity? What is yours? Have we considered our purpose as followers of Christ? Have we thought about why we're here or what we should be doing? These are important questions to ask, and the more we study the Scriptures to find the answers, the more we'll come to realize what this life is all about.

Something Bigger

"It's not about you," is the unforgettable first line from Rick Warren's book, *The Purpose Driven Life*. The reason we're here, the purpose for which we find ourselves existing on this earth, is much bigger than you and me. In fact, it's not about us, at all! We are here because of God and for God. When I come to understand the supreme power of my Creator and consider who I am in his presence, my spiritual perspective should change from one of self-importance to one of self-denial. I *need* God. I must have a relationship with him through his Son in order to have any hope at all. Without him, I am lost. Without me, he will continue to reign in Heaven for eternity. That's humbling.

It's not about me is exactly the lesson I learned early in my nursing career. It's about helping people recover from sickness and helping people stay well. It's about serving others in their times of need. It's about something much bigger than credentials. It's about my mission. It's about my purpose. It's about something deep in my heart that longs to make a difference in someone's life. Not because of any ability I have to heal, but because I can use my hands to clean a wound, or hold a cup of ice, or wipe a flushed face, or simply hold a hand. *It's not about me* is exactly the lesson I need to learn as a Christian.

Part of my job as a nursing supervisor involves verifying that each area of the hospital has the appropriate amount of staff on the schedule for the upcoming shift. A few weeks ago I was working a day shift at the hospital, and while I was making rounds on the oncology floor, I heard some yelling coming from a patient's room. I went in to see if everything was okay, and I found the patient, an elderly woman with her gown almost completely off, yelling and hitting at her daughter who was standing at the bedside.

The patient was clearly disoriented and upset. The charge nurse on the floor had entered the room right behind me, and together we fixed the patient's gown, pulled her up in bed, and fixed her covers. The whole time she was swatting at us, trying to bite us, and cursing at us, and her sweet daughter stood there softly crying and apologizing for her mother's behavior. We told her again and again that it was alright—we knew her mother was sick and not acting like her usual self. As for the patient, we just couldn't seem to calm her down. What the charge nurse did next brought tears to my eyes. She climbed into the bed next to the woman, began to stroke her hair, and whispered quietly next to her ear. The patient almost immediately became more relaxed and began to fall asleep.

I have no doubt that the charge nurse had 100 things she needed to be doing; I have no doubt that the patient was a complete stranger to her; I have no doubt that the patient is on that particular floor because she is battling some type of cancer; I have no doubt that the bed sheets in the patient's room had not been changed yet that day; I also have no doubt that what the nurse had on her mind was something bigger. That nurse carries in her heart a purpose: to care for people in need; and in that moment, a patient needed help, and she gave it in the best way she could. She wasn't thinking about herself at all, and through her actions, she painted a beautiful picture of selflessness.

I've gained immeasurable good from the profession I chose, but being able to witness the virtue of humility in nurses, patients, and family members has been the greatest blessing. Being around people with the *it's not about me* attitude has made me appreciate even more how important it is for me, as a Christian, to have the same sentiment as I walk daily in this sin-sick world.

What is Good

Humility. It conquers the greatest of sins—the sin of pride. In his book *Mere Christianity*, C.S. Lewis wrote, "It is pride which has been the chief cause of misery in every nation and every family since the world began." Pride may have been the sin that led to Satan's fall from Heaven. Pride is what caused Eve to eat the fruit in the Garden. Pride is what keeps so many people from surrendering their lives to God's will. Jesus listed pride among evil things that will cause us to be unclean or impure (Mark 7:21-23), and in Proverbs 6:16-19, pride is listed as one of the seven deadly sins. It's a sin that makes us feel as if we are better than others and that we deserve to be respected by others. Pride is the desire to lift ourselves up and hold ourselves in high esteem. We fight off pride when we practice humility.

I like this definition of humility: "a modest or low view of one's own importance." It's not that we aren't important; it's that we don't think too much of our importance. You've probably heard the saying, "Humility isn't thinking less of self; it's thinking of self...less!"

One Sunday morning, when Evie was a little girl, we were getting ready for worship and Sam took her to her room to help her get dressed. I had her new dress laid out with her matching shoes and hair bow. You'd think she would have been thrilled to put on her pretty outfit! *Nope.* She did *not* want to take off her pink princess pajamas! It must have been quite a show down! Sam came into our room again, shirt untucked and hair disheveled; followed by Evie, with a tear-streaked face and wearing a very wrinkled new dress. "Look Mommy! Daddy made me take off my princess 'jamma and now I'm just *regular* beautiful!"

Now, it wasn't that she wasn't beautiful anymore....she had just come down from *really*-beautiful to *regular*-beautiful. So cute, so pitiful, and so in need of a quick lesson on humility!

Being humble doesn't mean that we don't have value, but it is realizing that we are not valuable because of who we are or anything we've done. Value is not always intrinsic—it can also be bestowed on something because of the quality of the person to whom it belongs. In other words, we're not valuable because of who we are; we're valuable because we belong to God, and he has ascribed us our worth through the sacrifice of his Son. We're not valuable because of what we've done but because of the purpose God has assigned to us. Humility comes when we understand that.

To walk humbly with God is good. But how do we do it? If we are daily focusing our attention on the Lord, obeying him, allowing him to lead us, serving him and pleasing him, then humility should be our response. If we are walking by his side, we will see that he is righteous, that he is mighty, and that he is holy! Then, looking at ourselves, we will see weakness, sinfulness, and impurity. When I truly understand who he is and I truly understand who I am, the *only* way for me to walk with him is humbly.

A WALKING WARRIOR

We know him from the Bible as being a humble man, but Jesus said that *"among those born of women there has not risen one greater"* (Matthew

11:11). What was it about John Baptist that made our Lord and Savior refer to him as "the greatest"? Looking at his life, it's easy to see that there was nothing prideful about this devoted servant of God. The Scriptures reveal a subservient man who had been given the role of path-paver for the Messiah, not because of his goodness or hard work, but because God had graciously entrusted him with a unique purpose.

John the Baptist walked in humility. His entire life was lived in submission to God and in obedience to his will.

I think it came down to this: John understood who he was, and he understood who God is. He recognized that everything he was and everything that he had been given should be used for God's purpose to His glory. The way he lived reflected that! The Bible tells us repeatedly that the humble will be exalted (Psalm 147:6, Luke 14:11, James 4:10, 1 Peter 5:6). They will be lifted up! It may not happen in this fleshly life, but it will certainly happen in the everlasting spiritual one. I have no doubt that John has received his reward; and now, the years he spent as a humble messenger on this earth pave the way for me and you as we strive to walk selflessly day to day. When we look at his life through Scripture, here is what we learn from God's servant, John:

HE LIVED MEAGERLY.

"Now John himself was clothed in camel's hair, with a leather belt around his waist; and his food was locusts and wild honey" (Matthew 3:4).

"So the child grew and became strong in spirit, and was in the deserts till the day of his manifestation to Israel" (Luke 1:80).

"John answered and said, 'A man can receive nothing unless it has been given to him from Heaven'" (John 3:27).

HE SERVED AS A MINISTER.

"In those days John the Baptist came preaching in the wilderness of Judea, and saying, 'Repent, for the kingdom of heaven is at hand!'" (Matthew 3:1-2).

"Now it came to pass, as He was praying in a certain place, when He ceased,

that one of His disciples said to Him, 'Lord, teach us to pray, as John also taught his disciples'" (Luke 11:1).

HE UNDERSTOOD HIS MISSION.

"You yourselves bear me witness that I said, 'I am not the Christ, but I have been sent before Him. He who has the bride is the bridegroom; but the friend of the bridegroom, who stands and hears him, rejoices greatly because of the bridegroom's voice. Therefore, this joy of mine is fulfilled'" (John 3:28-29).

"And he preached saying, 'There comes One after me who is mightier than I, whose sandal strap I am not worthy to stoop down and loose'" (Mark 1:7).

HE SPENT HIS LIFE PAVING THE WAY FOR ANOTHER.

"He will also go before Him in the spirit and power of Elijah, 'to turn the hearts of the fathers to the children,' and the disobedient to the wisdom of the just, to make ready a people prepared for the Lord" (Luke 1:17).

"And you, child, will be called the prophet of the Highest; for you will go before the face of the Lord to prepare His ways, to give knowledge of salvation to His people by the remission of their sins, through the tender mercy of our God, with which the Dayspring from on high has visited us; to give light to those who sit in darkness and the shadow of death, to guide our feet into the way of peace" (Luke 1:76-79).

"There was a man sent from God, whose name was John. This man came for a witness, to bear witness of the Light, that all through him might believe, He was not that Light, but was sent to bear witness of that Light" (John 1:6-8).

HE NEVER REFERRED TO HIS OWN GREATNESS.

"He confessed and did not deny, but confessed, 'I am not the Christ.' And thy asked him, 'What are you then? Are you Elijah?' He said, 'I am not.' 'Are you the Prophet?' And he answered, 'No.' Then they said to him, 'Who are you then, that we may give an answer to those who sent us? What do you say about yourself?' He said, 'I am the voice of one crying in the wilderness: make *straight the way of the Lord.' As the prophet Isaiah has said"* (John 1:20-23).

"Then Jesus came from Galilee to John at the Jordan to be baptized by him. And John tried to prevent Him saying, 'I need to be baptized by You, and You are coming to me?'" (Matthew 3:13-14).

HE FADED FROM THE FOREFRONT WHEN IT WAS TIME.

"The next day John saw Jesus coming toward him, and said, 'Behold! The Lamb of God who takes away the sin of the world. This is He of whom I said, 'After me comes a Man who is preferred before me, for He was before me''" (John 1:29-30).

"He must increase, but I must decrease" (John 3:30).

A Beautiful Life-Collage

These are just snapshots of John the Baptist as we read about him in Scripture, but when we put them together, they create a beautiful collage of a life lived in humility. He was a man born with a God-given mission: to prepare the hearts and minds of people for the coming Messiah. He was filled with the Spirit from the time he was in his mother's womb and lived with the understanding that he had a special purpose. He lived modestly and served as a minister and prophet with a testimony that always centered on Christ. He spoke boldly and with conviction. He never elevated himself, nor did he desire the praise of man. He transferred all recognition and glory that he received to Jesus. And when his work was over, he stepped down. Just like that. The Messiah came, and John went. At the end, in the highest expression of selflessness, he gave his life for the cause of Christ. He humbly lived, he humbly died, and now he is exalted (Matthew 23:12)!

OUR DAILY WALK _____

I need God. He is my everything. I live because of him, I am not afraid of death because of him, I have hope for a home in Heaven because of him, I enjoy daily blessings because of him, and I gain strength through trials because of him. I know grace and mercy because of him. I love because of him.

IN HIS STEPS

In John 13:1-17, we read the beautiful account of Jesus washing the feet of his disciples—even the feet of Judas, the one who would betray him just hours later. What an amazing picture of submission and service Jesus painted for us in that moment. But truly, this characterized Jesus in every moment. His entire life was lived in humility and obedience. Everything he did was for the interest of others and never for himself. Oh, to be like him!

"Let this _____ be in you which was also in _____

_____, who being in the form of _____, did not consider

it robbery to be equal with God, but made Himself of no _____,

taking the form of a _____ - _____, and coming in the like-

ness of _____. And being found in _____ as a man, He

_____ Himself and became _____ to the point of

_____, even the death of the cross" (Philippians 2:5-8).

I need God because I will never be worthy of being called his child. I need him because he has promised me things that I could never achieve without him. I need him because I cannot win battles against Satan without His life-saving armor. I need God because without him I am a hopeless sinner.

I need God so desperately...but does God need *me*?

The simple answer is no; he doesn't. God does not *need* me. But the beautiful, inspiring truth that is revealed in the Bible is that God *wants* me. He doesn't *need* me, but he *wants* me! He wants me to live with him forever, he wants to give me good gifts, he wants to rain down blessings on me, and he wants to carry my burdens and to be a comfort to me.

And God wants me because he loves me.

But this is not just true for me.

God wants all people because he loves all people, and all people need him.

It's a beautiful truth!

The realization that I need God and the understanding that he is mindful of me at all should be enough for me to revoke any thought of self-importance and to keep me on my knees in humble gratitude.

When I daily turn my thoughts away from self, I can focus on doing good things for other people so that God can be glorified. I can stop worrying about my own esteem and work on building up others. I can recognize my own faults and ask for forgiveness, instead of pointing out the mistakes of others. With a spirit of humility, I seek peace, not vengeance; I speak courteously, not rudely; and I never pretend to be something I'm not.

To walk humbly is to be aware of the smallness of me compared to the greatness of God. It's to understand that nothing I have is mine and that everything I own comes from God, down to the minutes that make up the hours that make up my day. Humility is knowing that none of this is about me; it's *all* about God.

Strength

The Bible teaches us that there is much benefit to living a life that is "not about me." Read the following verses and write the blessing that will come from practicing humility.

James 4:6 –

Luke 14:11 –

Proverbs 22:4 –

Proverbs 11:2 –

Proverbs 18:12 –

Psalm 147:1:6 –

Matthew 5:3 –

Psalm 25:9 –

Isaiah 57:15 –

TRIALS

Humility can be difficult to practice in an "all about me" society. Someone who is humble might be accused of being weak or might experience different forms of persecution. We have to remember that there is nothing weak about being humble! Humility does not mean that we allow people to take advantage of us or harm us. Humility does not mean we hide our faith. Being humble does not prevent us from boldly taking a stand for what we believe.

Humility is submitting to the will of the Father. It's remembering who we are and why we are here. It's being obedient even when it's hard.

Read the story of the demon-possessed man found in Mark 5:1-20.

In verse 18, what did the formerly possessed man ask of Jesus?

What was Jesus' answer?

What was the man's response?

What can you and I learn about humility from this account?

ENCOURAGEMENT

I have worked in three different hospitals since graduating from Nursing School in 1996. These hospitals vary in their appearance, organization, and leadership; but one similarity that they each have is a unique Mission Statement. Each hospital, having patient care as its priority, has created a statement of focus for its employees so that everyone is aware of the ultimate goal of the facility.

I've wondered about my own personal Mission Statement. If someone asked me to recite mine, what would it be? Could I give an answer? As I thought about that one day I decided to go ahead and develop one. Here is what I came up with:

"Motivated by God's love for me as his child and the hope I have for a home in Heaven, I strive continually to imitate Jesus Christ in all that I say and do. In patterning my life after his, I will demonstrate more humility as a wife, mother, daughter, sister, and friend. With Christ as my example, and having a sincere desire that all should be saved, I will daily show his love to the people around me and share the message of the Gospel with others."

It's easy for me to become preoccupied with my busy day to day life. If I'm not careful, I can quickly get lost in myself: the things *I* need to do, the things *I* want to do, and the things that are important to *me*. I sometimes lose my focus, but my Mission Statement reminds me to reset the direction of my heart and steer my thoughts and attitude back to my God-given purpose.

Try creating your own Mission Statement. The Great Commission should be reflected in there somewhere! (Read Matthew 28:18-20 again for inspiration).

PRAYER

Mighty God, I come before you humbly in prayer with the sincere desire to be more like Jesus. I want to serve like him, love like him, and show kindness like him. Lead me to opportunities of service and guide me to people who need you.

Help me to think about myself less and think of others more. Help me to always remember that I am not better than anyone else, but I am a better person because of Christ.

Give me the strength to be submissive and the compassion to wash the feet of my friends and my enemies.

Thank you for your Son, whose obedience took him to the cross for me. Forgive me of my sins.

In Jesus' Name, Amen

WALK WITH THE DOC

Walking tip: Walk to de-stress

The complexities of modern society have led to stress becoming a major factor in disease causation. The mind (psyche) and body (soma) are inextricably linked. As a result, stress has become a major factor in the rise of so-called psychosomatic diseases. Many major diseases have a psychosomatic component – obesity, hypertension, diabetes, and even cancer. Stress and immunity are inversely related. As stress goes up, so does susceptibility to disease. There is a modicum of truth in the expressions, "You'll worry yourself sick" and "You'll work yourself to death." If fact, in Japan there is the term karoshi, which means suicide from overwork. These adverse effects of stress can be reduced substantially simply by walking, which reduces the levels of adrenalin and cortisol, the hormones responsible for those effects.

TAKE ACTION!

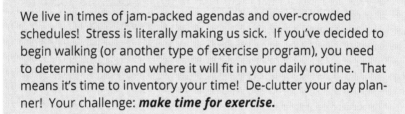

We live in times of jam-packed agendas and over-crowded schedules! Stress is literally making us sick. If you've decided to begin walking (or another type of exercise program), you need to determine how and where it will fit in your daily routine. That means it's time to inventory your time! De-clutter your day planner! Your challenge: ***make time for exercise.***

CHAPTER FIVE

WATCH WHERE YOU STEP
Walk Carefully

"See then that you walk circumspectly, not as fools but as wise, redeeming the time, because the days are evil. Therefore, do not be unwise, but understand what the will of the Lord is" (Ephesians 5:15-16).

*H*ow do you spell the word caution?" Kate yelled from the kitchen. My husband, Sam, spelled it out for her and not another word was said.

Later, when Sam walked into the kitchen, he found a spill on the floor and next to the spill was a handmade sign that read:

Caution!

WET FLOOR!

(Beneath that warning, there was an ominous picture of a little stick man slipping in a mysterious puddle, just to send home the message).

Sam asked me to join him in the kitchen, we had quite a laugh, I took a picture of the sign (like a good mom), and then we called our daughter to come clean up the mess.

After complimenting her creativity, we explained to Kate that she could have wiped up the spill and been well on her way to other things in less time than it took for her to create the sign! Even though its original purpose was to ensure the safety of others, the sign served as a constant reminder of her "Saturday Afternoon Sweet Tea Disaster." Every time she walked through the kitchen the sign would be there, with its little stick man taunting and chiding in a sing-song voice, *"You made a me-ss...you made a me-ss!"* How much better it would have been for her to have just cleaned it up and moved on!

We also talked to Kate about how to be more careful when pouring herself a cup of sweet tea the next time: Don't set the cup right next to the edge of the counter, hold the pitcher with two hands, try not to fill the cup to the very tip-top. If you accidentally spill some, don't just leave the mess! Grab a towel, clean it up, and ask for help if you need it. Then, try again!

That night, I thought about the sign (which has now found itself among our collection of paper keepsakes), and it reminded me of how Christians sometimes live day to day and how we often treat sin in our lives. I wonder how much thought we put into living *carefully* so that we can keep a sin-spill from ever happening? Do we know the instructions God has given us to help us avoid sticky-situations? Do we follow them?

Sometimes we aren't careful, and we sin. Sometimes we try really hard to be careful, and we still mess up. When that happens, we're pretty good at acknowledging our mistakes; we may even call attention to them around others, but when it comes to "cleaning up the spill," sometimes we don't make the effort. We leave signs next to our behaviors that say "Caution! Sin!" but then we leave the mess there, getting stickier and stickier, putting us (and others in our lives) at risk for slipping.

An important aspect of careful Christian living is being a good custodian! If we have a sin-spill, we can clean up our lives again through repentance and prayer. We can't just be sorry about our sin; we have to commit to making a complete change in our behavior, which may require getting rid of negative influences that can lead us to sin. Then we can protect ourselves from future "spills" by waxing our hearts with Bible words because knowing what God wants you to do is good spill prevention, and it makes clean-up easier when necessary. As Christians, we never stop "spilling," but we can learn how to be more careful in the kitchen and how to become better custodians!

Carefully Look

The letter that Paul wrote to the church in Ephesus follows the same pattern as many of his other epistles. The first half of the letter deals with doctrinal teaching, while the second half involves practical application of that teaching. In this particular letter, Paul spends chapters 1-3 talking to the Ephesians about being "in Christ" and the significance of that relationship. For chapters 4-6, it's as if Paul said, "I've told you who you are, and now this is how you should live." He specifically wrote to them about different aspects of the Christian walk and provided instructions on how to step.

In Ephesians 5:15, Paul tells his readers to "walk circumspectly." This word "circumspectly" has a very interesting meaning. It comes from the Latin element *circum-* meaning "around, round about," or literally "in a circle," along with the Latin word *specere,* meaning "to look at." Putting the two together, we have a word that means "to look around" or "to look in a circle."

In your mind, picture a person walking down a path. As she is walking, her head is turning to the right and to the left; she's looking behind as well as ahead. You would say that this person is carefully watching where she is going, but not only that, she is also carefully aware of everything that is happening around her. This is how Paul was telling the Christians in Ephesus to live. Live carefully! Look all around you as you go!

One night I was working at the hospital, and I received a call from a very unhappy family member. Her father was a patient and had wrapped his dentures up in a napkin and set them on his bedside table. Now they were missing. She felt pretty sure they had been unintentionally thrown away by one of our staff members. I understood her frustration because dentures are not cheap! I assured her that I would do my best to try and find them.

I started by checking with the environmental services team. As it turned out, an associate had recently finished the routine cleaning of that floor, and she had just taken the trash bags to the large receptacles outside of the hospital. She showed me exactly where her load of bags had been dumped, and as I stood there staring at all the tied up plastic bags, I thought, "*This is gross* AND *I'm never going to find those teeth.*" But with a large dose of the humility I talked about in the last chapter (and a healthy respect for patient satisfaction scores), I grabbed some gloves and began sorting.

Talk about "circumspectly"! I have never looked around more deliberately than I did as I dug through that trash. What if someone had accidently thrown a needle away? What if there was some infectious body fluid that had ended up in the wrong place? Each bundled up napkin held a potential treasure or a potential danger! Dumpster Diving for Dentures proved to be a task that took time and careful attention.

Unbelievably, I found those teeth! It was a happy ending for everyone, and for me, a lesson well learned on exactly what Paul meant when he told Christians to "walk circumspectly."

Carefully Listen

Careful walking involves a visual awareness of what is going on all around us, but it also involves listening. When I think of careful listening, I remember a story found in 1 Kings 19 about one of God's prophets.

Elijah had every reason to be afraid, and he desperately needed God's guidance. At one point, he had been pleading with the Israelites to turn back to God and honor their divine covenant; he was running from the evil queen Jezebel who had threatened to have him killed; he had been forty days and forty nights without food, and he was sleeping in a cave on Mount Horeb waiting to hear from God.

Elijah was called to come out of the cave and to stand on the mountain before the Lord.

A strong wind came…but the Lord was not in the wind.

After the wind, an earthquake shook the mountain…but the Lord was not in the earthquake.

After the earthquake there came a fire…but the Lord was not in the fire.

After the fire…there was a *still, small voice.*

When Elijah heard the voice, he wrapped his cloak around his face, stood at the entrance of the cave, and then received his instructions from the Lord.

God spoke to Elijah in a gentle whisper…and Elijah was listening.

Sometimes, I believe God might be quietly telling us something, but all we hear are the loud, mountain-shaking things going on around us. Sometimes, maybe, we just need to carefully listen.

There are times we look to God for direction. We beg him for it in our prayers. We want to know what we should do with our lives or how we should handle a certain situation. We may feel worried or afraid. We go to God with lists of questions or requests and then wait, sometimes impatiently, for his answers to reveal themselves. We might even get frustrated wondering if our prayers are being heard. We hurry through our busy days, talking to God on the run, but never really stopping long enough to listen for his response.

God speaks to us from his Word, but we can also hear him through the loving support of our family, through the kindness of our friends, through the innocence of our children, through the comforting words of a song, or through the peaceful beauty of nature. God gently whispers to us, reminding us that he loves us, that he is near, and that he has a plan for us. If we will take time every day to slow down and be mindful of the still, small voice of God, we might find that he has been answering our prayers all along.

Carefully Live

We can walk carefully by looking all around us and by listening for direction, but neither of those things will help us if we don't know what we are looking or listening *for*. In order to carefully live our daily lives, we have to know God's instruction. We have to know his expectations and guidelines. It's the only way to distinguish the treasures from the dangers as we sort through life…because sometimes, on the outside, they both look like a crumpled up napkin!

In the Air Force my dad had the opportunity to fly many different types of aircraft. I remember him walking through the door at the end of the day wearing his flight suit and how my sisters and I would run into his arms and pull off all of his patches! (It's funny how a memory so simple can be one of the most precious). Part of being a pilot involves completing the pre-flight checklist to ensure that everything is ready and in order for a safe flight. *Flight controls…check! Fuel quantity…check!* I imagine my Dad sitting in a cock-pit and meticulously reviewing those lists every time he flew an airplane. I see him pushing buttons and flipping switches over his head, scanning the instrument panel in front of him, turning dials, and checking numbers. It's a process that requires careful attention because if something is not where it should be or not performing properly, then the flight will be delayed until everything is re-checked, repaired, and all systems are go.

A careful walk involves a routine review of our standard, which is the Word of God. We have to check ourselves to be certain we are living according to his will so that we can travel safely and be well prepared if we should experience turbulence. God's Word also teaches us how we need to live in order to avoid a sin-spill, it helps us identify potential hazards as we daily walk, and it provides us direction and a means of determining what is true. To carefully live, we have to carefully study the Bible.

A WALKING WARRIOR

"For Ezra had prepared his heart to seek the Law of the Lord, and to do it, and to teach statutes and ordinances in Israel" (Ezra 7:10). This verse paints a beautiful picture of a man who had dedicated himself to doing the will of God. The next verse describes him as "a priest, a scribe, and an expert in the words of the commandments of the Lord and of His statutes to Israel." Ezra was a "walking warrior" who carefully studied, taught, and wrote copies of the Word of God.

In 538 B.C., under the decree of King Cyrus of Persia, the Jews had been allowed to leave Babylon to return to their homeland after seventy years of captivity. Not only had the king ordered their return, he also encouraged the rebuilding of the temple in Jerusalem and provided funding for the costs of travel and reconstruction! Once again, God fulfilled his plan using the most unlikely people. God keeps his Word! He had promised restoration, and restoration came—by the hands of secular leaders.

The return from exile took place in three stages, just as the people of Judah had been taken captive in three stages. The first stage of return began in 538 B.C. and was led by Zerubbabel, the governor of Judah, who began the work of rebuilding the temple of God. The second stage took place in 458 B.C. and was led by Ezra, whose focus was rebuilding the spiritual lives of the people through teaching the Law and purifying their worship. In 444 B.C., the third and final stage occurred under the leadership of Nehemiah, who rebuilt the walls of Jerusalem and enabled the people to re-inhabit the city. Rebuild and restore was the rallying cry of God's people!

We first meet Ezra in the book that bears his name. In the reign of King Artaxerxes, Ezra was given permission to take a second group of Israelites back to Jerusalem. When he arrived there, he found that the people had fallen to an alarming spiritual low. They had intermarried with pagan nations and had forgotten their spiritual heritage. Ezra immediately humbled himself before God, prayed for the forgiveness of the people, and then began a wave of spiritual reform throughout the land.

Nearly fifteen years later, Nehemiah returned to Jerusalem with the third group of exiles and began reconstructing the walls of the city against considerable odds. Through the work of God, the wall was completed in fifty-two days, and the stage was set for a momentous spiritual revival. In the eighth chapter of Nehemiah, we find the children of Israel gathered together in Jerusalem, with open ears and willing hearts, ready for restoration, and eager to hear the Word of God read by Ezra the scribe.

A Careful Handling of Scripture

Almost one thousand years before, the Israelites had been commanded by God to read the Law every seven years. This was so they could learn to fear him and *"carefully observe all the words of this Law."* It was also so their children could learn it and come to fear God (Deuteronomy 31:11-13). The same command had been given to their king that *"he may learn to fear the Lord his God and be careful to observe all the words of this law and these statutes, that his heart may not be lifted above his brethren, that he may not turn aside from the commandment to the right hand of to the left"* (Deuteronomy 17:14-20). God expected his Law to be carefully followed.

Ezra read from the Book of the Law from morning until mid-day, and the way in which the Israelite men and women responded serves as an excellent example of how we should carefully handle the Word of God today.

LISTEN TO THE WORD. Ezra stood before all of those who could hear with understanding and began to read the Law. In verse 3, we are told that the "ears of all the people were attentive to the Book of the Law." They listened carefully!

HAVE RESPECT FOR THE WORD. In verses 5 and 6, we see the reverence expressed by the Israelites for the Law. The people stood up as the book was opened. They lifted their hands and answered "Amen, Amen!" Then they bowed with their faces to the ground and worshiped the Lord. They were respectful!

UNDERSTAND THE TRUTH OF THE WORD. The people had the Law explained to them in a way that made sense and helped them comprehend what had been read. They went to trusted religious leaders for guidance and direction. The truth convicted them, and they wept over the words of the Law. They gained understanding!

BE OBEDIENT TO THE WORD. During the reading of the Law, the Israelites discovered it had been commanded by Moses that they live in temporary booths, or hut-type shelters, during the Feast of Tabernacles. They hadn't observed that religious practice since the days of Joshua, one thousand years earlier! Immediately, they went out and collected the branches needed for making the booths and restored what had been lost for so many years (vv. 14-17). They were obedient!

From the account found in Nehemiah 8, we find the careful handling of God's Word involves listening to his Law, respecting his Law, understanding his Law, and obeying his Law.

IN HIS STEPS

Jesus knew the will of his Father, and he lived it continually. Everything he did was according to God's authority. In John 7:16, when the Jews marveled at his teaching, Jesus told them, "My doctrine is not mine, but His that sent me."

Even the words he spoke were by the command of his Father. In John 12:49-50, he cried out because of the unbelievers saying,

"For I have not spoken on My own _____ but the _____ who sent Me gave Me a command, what I should _____ and what I should _____. And I know that His command is _____ _____. Therefore, whatever I _____, just as the Father has told Me, so I _____."

I remember as a child sitting with my mom one day while she was talking to me about the Bible. I'll never forget her saying, "Lori, when you are saying your prayers, always ask God to give you wisdom. He has promised to give it to those who ask and who believe that he will." Ever since that day, I have prayed for the wisdom that comes from God.

I pray that he will grant me wisdom as a wife and as a mother. I pray for wisdom concerning the subjects on which I am asked to write or speak. I pray for wisdom when teaching classes, when working at the hospital, and before I answer difficult, heart-wrenching, soul-searching questions. I also regularly pray for wisdom when it comes to reading, studying, and applying the Word of God in my life every day.

I pray for wisdom because I don't have all the answers. I pray for it because I want to truly live the way the Bible tells me I should live. I pray for it because I am human, and I need God's help.

Let me encourage you to ask for wisdom in your daily prayers. Ask for the wisdom that will keep you away from temptations and help you carefully look, listen, and live according to God's Word.

We should also redeem the time, or as it's translated in the NASB: *make the most of our time.* This means taking advantage of opportunities as we encounter them, especially those opportunities that allow us to do good in this evil world.

We live carefully by knowing the will of the Lord and being filled with, or led by, the Spirit. Both of these involve studying, understanding, and applying God's Word. We come to know the will of God through his Word, and we are led by the Spirit through his Word. Careful Christians are vigilant when it comes to Bible study. Remember the Bereans (Acts 17:11)!

STRENGTH

How can you become a more carefully walking Christian?

In what ways can you carefully listen to the voice of God?

Consider the Israelites' response to the reading of the Law. How do you carefully handle God's Word?

TRIALS

The devil is deceptive. He camouflages sin. He can make it look good, or seem like "no big deal." He has scattered it all around us and disguised it as entertainment, friendship, and even love. We have to be watchful, always looking, always mindful of the dangers that might be lurking around us.

What daily dangers do you encounter that require careful looking?

We all experience sin-spills in our lives. Sometimes these are just occasional slip-ups that we can fix ourselves through personal prayer, but sometimes they can become habitual, and we might need more help.

The Bible encourages repentance and prayer. It encourages us to confess our faults to each other. How well do you think we do this as Christians? (If your answer is "not so well" or "we could do better," what do you think we can do to improve? Would improving in this area help or hurt the church?)

ENCOURAGEMENT

The opposite of living carefully is living dangerously. It is dangerous to live without the knowledge of God's Word. It's also dangerous to know it and not obey it. We have to be intentional when it comes to walking carefully through the wilderness. One way we can promote safe travel is to plan and implement a Bible study and prayer schedule. In order to help you get started, think about your answers to these questions:

1. *What is your purpose for reading the Bible?*
2. *What time of your day works best for personal Bible study?*
3. *Would this also be a good time for prayer, or do you need to plan a separate time for the purpose of talking deeply and privately with God?*
4. *How often would you like to read and study the Bible?*
5. *Where is a comfortable place for you to read?*
6. *Is this also the best place for you to pray? If not, where is the most comfortable place for your prayer time? (Prayer continues throughout the day, but this is a time for uninterrupted, focused, and personal fellowship between you and your Heavenly Father)*
7. *How much time would you like to spend reading the Bible?*
8. *What is your goal?*
9. *What can you do to increase your learning and retention?*
10. *What can you do when your mind wanders?*

Now grab a calendar! Pick a time slot each day for the next seven days that you will dedicate to prayer and Bible study. If you miss a day, do not despair and don't quit! Forgive yourself and start again the next day. At the end of seven days, plan your next two weeks. Keep on planning. Keep on studying. Keep on praying.

PRAYER

Dear Lord, help me to carefully consider where I am walking and how I am walking. Be with me as I look, listen, and live in this world and guide me on the path that will lead me to the Promised Land.

Grant me wisdom, opportunities, and understanding of your Will. I pray that I will be led by your Spirit.

My heart is set on carefully handling your Word. I desire to hear it, respect it, understand it, and obey it. Help me, Lord.

Hold me in your hand and keep me from evil.

In Jesus' Name, Amen

WALK WITH THE DOC

Walking tip: Walk for balance

Walking is an excellent means of developing and maintaining one's sense of balance. The major elements of the balance mechanism, the eyes, inner ear, and sensory receptors in the muscles and joints, are kept well-honed by walking. Living a sedentary lifestyle, particularly during the later years when there has been age-related loss of lean mass will be setting you up for a fall, which can be debilitating, and even life threatening. A well-established walking program combined with some resistance training for upper body will substantially reduce the risk of falling.

TAKE ACTION!

How is your sense of balance? There are simple ways that you can evaluate your balance at home. With a quick Internet search you'll find a number of websites with step-by-step instructions for performing a variety of balance tests. Try a few and see how you do!

CHAPTER SIX

KEEP ON KEEPING ON

Walk by Faith

"*For we walk by faith, not by sight*" (2 Corinthians 5:7).

Every year my sisters, my dad, and I travel to Wright-Patterson Air Force Base in Dayton, Ohio to participate in the Air Force Half Marathon. We have deemed this event an "annual family tradition," complete with matching T-shirts to wear on race day and 1732 digitally preserved moments of gut-busting hilarity by the end of the weekend.

When it comes to a half-marathon, we join the ranks of the "walkers." We keep a steady pace for the duration of the course and are quite content being left in the dust of the pacers and qualifiers. I enjoy training and conditioning for a run, and even have a hankering for the competition from time to time, but when I'm with my family at one of these events, we hit the pavement for a different purpose. To us, the half-marathon is about the fellowship, the laughter, and the bonding. It's 13.1 miles of precious memory making.

It's different, though, when it comes to the spiritual race we run as Christians. Paul admonished the church in Corinth that in regard to this race, they should be "in it to win it" (1 Corinthians 9:24), and the writer of Hebrews tells us that we should "*run with endurance the race that is before us, fixing our eyes on Jesus*" (Hebrews 12:1-2). The Christian race requires discipline and training. In this race, the purpose is to win the prize, which is only reserved for those faithful runners whose hearts are focused on staying the course.

Life's course is not an easy one. Orange cones don't line the way making it obvious the direction we should go, rather we determine the course through careful Bible study and constant prayer. Sometimes the road is rough, sometimes we feel like dropping out of the race, and sometimes the prize at the end seems unobtainable: those are the times when it really helps to be surrounded by family and friends who share a common goal. I've learned from these half-marathons that sometimes we can face difficulties on our own, but sometimes we can't.

One year, Dad, Jenny, Julia, and I found ourselves walking behind an older gentleman. His gray tipped "high and tight" and his T-shirt sporting the letters USMC, gave him away as being retired military. He shuffled along, sweat dripping off his face, eyes locked on the pavement ahead, when all of a sudden something in his path caused him to trip. He fell, full impact, to the ground. My dad rushed over to offer help, but the man stopped him abruptly with an upheld palm, and with all confidence stated, "I've got this." He stood up, blood coming from scratches on his head, arms, and legs and restarted his shuffle to the finish line. Dad turned to me and my sisters and said, "Now that is one tough fella!" Sometimes, in life, when we fall along the course we can honestly say, "I've got this," and we just get up and keep going.

On the other hand, sometimes we need the help of others in order to stay on track. There is nothing more motivating at a marathon than to witness runners with visual challenges participating in the event. At times, these individuals will run in the center of a protective circle of friends who will guide them around obstacles and keep them within bounds. Other times, they run with a partner, and the two will be connected by a rope, or a bar, or will even hold opposite ends of a towel in order to share vision on the course and safely reach the finish line. Occasionally, from behind you'll hear the shout, "Runner, coming through!" and immediately the crowd will heed the voice of the caller and clear a passage for the team who represents such a spirit of unity, strength, and endurance.

Life is a race that we enter to win and we don't quit! Challenges arise, like potholes or cracks in the blacktop, and whether we stagger alone with road rash or reach out to fellow runners when we lose sight of the path, we keep on keeping on! The true joy will be crossing the finish line where the prize awaits! Then we will be able to say like Paul in 2 Timothy 4:7-8, *"I have fought the good fight, I have finished the course, I have kept the faith; in the future there is laid up for me the crown of righteousness, which the Lord, the righteous Judge, will award to me on that day; and not only to me, but also to all who have loved His appearing."*

When Times are Good

Faith is a little easier to have when manna is falling from the sky every morning or when your belly is full and water is flowing from the rock. It's not hard to walk in faith when the path is smooth and there is no sign of trouble around you. It's simple to trust in God when everything seems to be going according to your plan, right? Well, not always.

Sometimes when life is smooth sailing, our faith ends up in the storage area below deck. We find ourselves standing at the helm, peacefully steering our boat and thinking, "This is a piece of cake!" We begin to feel like capable captains, pretty confident on the course we've set. We might look out over the calm waters and think about how lucky we are to have such a sturdy boat and how we've chosen quite the perfect place to sail. Is it possible for things to go so well that we completely neglect our faith?

When times are good, we might find our faith comes easy. The schedule is full, but not overwhelming. The jobs are busy, but not stressful. The family is active, but not chaotic. The house is clean, the people closest to us are healthy, and there's money in the bank! Everything's going well, and on top of that, we have all kinds of time to spend in Bible study and prayer. We are thankful to God for his blessings and our faith is growing by leaps and bounds.

But, when times are good we also might find that our faith takes a back seat. Our lives are going so well that we forget about God. We forget that the blessings we have come from him. We forget that he holds in his hand the very sea on which we are peacefully sailing. It might be that while the good times are rolling along, we get so wrapped up in our personal happiness that we roll God right out of the picture. Our Bibles stay on the bookshelves and our prayer closets stay closed, because we suddenly forget that we need God.

We can choose one of these two different responses: faith growing stronger, or faith becoming weaker. Think about your life for just a moment. When times are good what happens to your faith?"

While you're thinking about that, here's another question to consider: *What happens when your life isn't going well at all?*

When Times are Hard

Our wilderness walk is not a walk in the park. It can be difficult. It can be downright scary, and it can be deeply painful. When those hard times come, just like in the good times, our faith will respond in one way or another.

Picture the same boat sailing on smooth waters. Now imagine that dark clouds appear out of nowhere and rain begins to fall; the winds bolster and thunder rumbles overhead. The boat begins to struggle as the water becomes rougher and the waves rise higher. It's difficult to hold onto the helm, and it becomes obvious that you're not strong enough to keep the boat on course, or even above water for that matter. You need help. In fact, you need saving.

As the boat is rocking and tossing in the storm, you hear a crash below deck and know that the cargo has been scattered everywhere. Taking a quick glance down into the cabin you see a crate on the floor marked with the word: "FAITH." *How did that get down there?* You walk down the steps holding tightly to the rail, grab the "faith" crate, and bring it back up on deck. Inside there is an instruction manual with a message on the cover that reads, "For use with anchor."

An anchor. A flash of lightning illuminates the sky for just a moment and your eyes are drawn to a glint at the bow of the ship. A chain! Leaning into the wind, shielding your face from the sting of the rain, with heavy footsteps you walk carefully toward the chain, to the place where an anchor is waiting. There is hope! If you anchor down, you stay on course. If you stay on course, you can find your way home again.

Faith has been restored. With the instruction manual in hand, you lay hold of the anchor that will get you through this storm. As you lower it down, you find that it doesn't rest on the floor of the sea; instead, it fastens in the very presence of God who holds it all—the sea, the storm, the boat—all of it, in the palm of his hand. You realize that God has been there all along—in the smooth sailing and now in the storm. You invite him to take over as captain; not just for the duration of the tempest, but for the duration of the journey.

In the storm, it's easy to see that we need help. It's easy to rely on God when we've gone as far as we can go. It's easy to believe in God when we are in desperate need of being saved.

That's not what happened with the Israelites though. When times got hard, they walked away from God. When there was no food, they complained; when they were thirsty, they cried out. When God took too long, they turned to other gods. When the wilderness tried them with its scorpions and sand dunes, their faith crumbled.

We can choose one of these two different responses: faith growing stronger, or faith becoming weaker. Think about your life for just a moment. When times are hard what happens to your faith?"

Then there are those times of uncertainty. *What happens then?*

When Times are Uncertain

I'll be honest. Sometimes I'm afraid. Sometimes I worry. Sometimes I "what-if" myself into a silent panic or cry over the aftermath of something that has not even happened. Sometimes, I feel helpless over what is going on in the world around me, and I agonize over the future. I pray desperate prayers over my children. Sometimes, when I fall into bed at night I am worn out from playing spiritual Red Rover against adversity all day long. *"Red Rover, Red Rover, send 'doubting' right over."* And in my mind, my hands and arms are aching after being pummeled again and again. *"Send 'fearful' right over...Send 'guilty' right over..."* My team has shrunk with every broken link, and the enemy that is standing on the opposite side of the playground has taken captive my friends: happiness, peace, and courage.

It's exhausting.

It's exhausting, and it's not spiritually healthy.

It's exhausting, it's not spiritually healthy, and it's not what God wants.

God does not want us to be afraid. He does not want us to worry. He does not want us to feel helpless. He does not want our fear, or uncertainty, to overcome our faith.

The truth that we read in the Bible is that God wants us to be filled with hope. He wants us to have joy. He wants us to stay strong, to shine his light in this world, and to know with certainty that he is always with us!

We need to reflect every morning on the fact that we are not from here. We must remind ourselves more often about what it means to be a child of God. Our future is firmly planted in Heaven with my Father who is waiting for us to come home, and one day we will be in that wonderful place, where there will be no fear, no worry, no pain, and no tears.

We have to refocus on where we're going to live eternally rather than where we're living today. *That* will keep us strong. *That* will help us stand up for the Truth without fear. *That* will motivate us to love deeper. *That* will help reframe our prayers of desperation into prayers of faith.

I should keep in mind when I visit my unseen playground that God is standing next to me in the Red Rover line. He is on *my* team, and he is holding *my* hand so tightly that nothing—*absolutely nothing*—can break our chain! He sends me running toward the enemy empowered with his Word, and I crash through their line, rescuing happiness…and then peace….and then courage. Then, when doubt or fear come running full force in our direction, they will hit our firmly clasped hands and simply fall. God won't allow them to join our team. He will send them back where they came from with the reminder that they can keep trying, but when it's all said and done, they've already lost.

At All Times

We need to remember that faith is acting, thinking, and speaking based on what we know to be true, not on what we might be feeling at a given moment.

Faith is not a blind leap; it's following the light of God's Word.

Faith is daily dependence on God in all things, at all times.

A WALKING WARRIOR

In 1 Kings 17:7-16, we read a story about a widow. We never know her name, only that she lived in the city of Zarephath, which was located outside of Israel in the territory of Phoenicia—the home country of the wicked Jezebel. It was a place of idol worship and wide-spread corruption, but God had plans to use one of its poorest citizens in a mighty and providential way.

Elijah lived as a prophet in Israel during the reign of the evil duo, King Ahab and Queen Jezebel. Under their rule, wickedness filled the land and idolatry was rampant. God's people had turned away from him, and as a result, famine and drought spread throughout the land. The Lord sent Elijah to hide by the Brook Cherith where he was fed bread and meat by ravens and drank water from the brook. When the waters of Cherith dried up, Elijah received word from the Lord that he should go to Zarephath to live, and there he would find a widow to provide for his needs.

I've chosen the Widow of Zarephath as our warrior who walked by faith, but Elijah certainly deserves warrior status as well! He did exactly what God told him to do even when it meant seeking refuge in a heathen country, not knowing where he would live or what he would eat, and with the understanding that a widow would be the one to care for him. Elijah's tremendous faith is seen in these seven words that begin 1 Kings 17:10, *"So he arose and went to Zarephath."* Although he didn't know how, Elijah believed that God would provide. And God did—in the most unlikely, unpredictable of ways.

From Poverty, Hopelessness, and Unbelief

When Elijah first approached the city of Zarephath, God's providence was already at work! At the gate of the city, a widow was collecting sticks. She didn't "just happen" to be there; God's unseen hand was pulling everything together for the good of Elijah and the widow, too. Elijah asked her for water; and as she turned to go and get it, he called out for her to also bring him some bread to eat.

In verse 12 of the text, we learn more about this widow. She responded to Elijah with these words, *"As the Lord your God lives, I do not have bread, only a handful of flour in a bin, and a little oil in a jar; and see, I am gathering a couple of sticks that I may go in and prepare it for myself and my son, that we may eat it, and die."*

We learn that she was poor. She only had a handful of flour and a small amount of oil. This was the last bit of food she possessed.

We learn that she was in a state of hopelessness. She believed that she and her son would be eating their final meal. She fully expected that they both would die.

We learn that she was not a child of God. When she spoke to Elijah, she began by saying, *"the Lord **your** God,"* not indicating any personal relationship with him. Remember, she lived in a Gentile city that was overrun with idol worship.

How could God possibly use a poor, hopeless, unbelieving Gentile widow to take care of his prophet? Elijah may have been wondering the exact same thing! But God doesn't always work in the ways you and I would expect, or want. Elijah surely didn't expect for ravens to feed him, and he surely had no desire to ask a desperate widow for help, but God knew what He was doing. As Elijah's circumstances seemed to pull him lower and lower, God was continuing a work of faith in him that was growing and growing. Although he didn't know it at the time, Elijah was being prepared for an epic showdown with the prophets of Baal (1 Kings 18). God would need Elijah's faith to be unwavering; ravens and a despairing widow were part of the plan to get him there.

God might sometimes take us all the way to the point of thinking "it can't get any worse," because those desperate moments become our places of surrender. It's in those moments that we finally say, "I'm turning it all over to you, God, because there's nothing more I can do." When we reach that point, and arrive in that place, God says, "Trust Me. I'm preparing you for something greater."

So far, this story has already shown us that God will use unlikely people or circumstances to accomplish his will. But there's more! Sometimes the tests that God puts in our lives are not only to build up our own faith, but to also influence the faith of someone else. That's exactly what we see happen to the widow of Zarephath!

To Provision, Blessing, and Testimony

Not only did Elijah ask for food from the widow, he also asked for her to make him a small cake first—before she made anything for herself or her son. The widow must have been shocked at his request! She only had enough for her and for her son to have one serving each, and this man was asking her to make him something *first*. That would mean either she or her son would have to go without. As a mother, there is no question that I would choose to feed my children before myself, and I imagine she might have felt the same way. If so, she would be forfeiting her last meal in order to feed her son and a stranger. But Elijah made her this promise, *"For thus says the Lord God of Israel: 'The bin of flour shall not be used up, nor shall the jar of oil run dry, until the day the Lord sends rain on the earth."*

In other words: if you do this, God will take care of your needs. So she went and did what Elijah had asked. In verses 14-15, we read what happened as a result of her faithful obedience: *"...and she and he and her household ate for many days. The bin of flour was not used up, nor did the jar of oil run dry, according to the word of the Lord, which He spoke by Elijah."*

The widow acted in faith, and she was blessed. What if she hadn't helped Elijah? Would she have received the blessing of daily food to last the remainder of the drought? Would she and her son have died? There were two ways the widow could have handled the situation: feed Elijah to receive an inconceivable blessing or turn him away and have the assurance of one last meal with her son. She chose to step out in faith. What a lesson for us! When we are faced with a difficult trial, remember: our response to that test will determine what's next. God will provide for the faithful.

The story doesn't end there! Another trial tested the faith of the widow. In verse 17, we find that her son became sick, and the illness was so severe that it took his life. She went to Elijah and said, *"What have I to do with you, O man of God? Have you come to me to bring my sin to remembrance, and to kill my son?"*

Did she think she was being judged for her sins? Did she think that she was being punished by the death of her son? We don't know what was going through her mind, but it's clear that she was in agony. Why would her son have been saved from starvation, only to lose his life a short time later? She thought it must have been because of something she had done in her past. Elijah simply said, *"Give me your son."*

He took the child to the upper room where he was staying and laid him on the bed. He stretched himself out on the child three times and prayed to God that the child's soul would come back to him. The Lord heard Elijah and the child's life was restored. Elijah took him to his mother and said, *"See, your son lives!"* Her faith was restored! Her pain turned to praise! She rejoiced and responded saying, *"Now by this I know that you are a man of God, and that the word of the Lord in your mouth is the truth."*

Jesus mentioned her when he spoke in the synagogue in Nazareth at the beginning of his ministry (Luke 4:24-27). He proclaimed that in the same way that she had received God's blessing because of her faith, the Gentile people would also receive God's blessing because of their faith! Then, in Hebrews 11:35, tucked into the list of people having *"obtained a good testimony through faith,"* there could very well be a reference to the widow of Zarephath with the words *"women received their dead raised to life again."*

The miracle involving the widow's son is the first resurrection recorded in Scripture and continues to instill hope in the hearts of those who read her story. Her life is a testimony to God's providence, a testimony to the blessings that come through faith, and a testimony to God's mercy which has been shown to all people. From the moment Elijah stepped into her world, she walked by faith and not by sight.

IN HIS STEPS

Jesus is the greatest hero of faith to ever have lived. His faith in God is portrayed throughout the New Testament, from the life of submission he lived until the time of his cruel death on the cross. With his first recorded words, "Why did you seek Me? Did you not know that I must be about My Father's business?" to his final words, "It is finished," Jesus demonstrated complete trust in God and obedience to his will. He is both our perfect object of faith and our perfect example of faith.

Read Hebrews 12:1-2. This verse tells us that we are to,

"...run with endurance the race that is set before us, looking unto Jesus, the

_____ and _____ of our faith..."

Daily walking by faith is a decision we make. We decide that we are going to remain faithful regardless of what we encounter in the wilderness. We decide that we are going to do God's will, even when it's hard or even when we may not feel like it. Jesus lived in faithful obedience to God every day of his life, knowing how it would end on the hill of Mount Calvary. He could have quit at any moment, but he decided differently. He decided to go to the cross. Jesus chose faith.

It's not easy. It involves trust. Sometimes we don't know what's waiting for us around the corner. We don't know what tomorrow has in store. Like in the wilderness, one moment we might be cooling off our feet in the waters of a desert oasis, and the next moment we might be choking on the sands of a desert storm. Life changes, in good and in terrible ways. In this physical world there is not much we can control, but this is certain—*you* control your faith. Hold onto it fiercely.

There will be days when we might think about giving up. Bailing out. Buckling under. As battered boxers, we might almost be ready to throw in the towel. Hold out for the end of the round! There's a coach waiting in the corner of the ring with a squirt of water and 60 seconds of "don't give ups" and "you can do its!"

We need that time in the corner with our Coach. We fight round after round after round, and sometimes we get pretty beaten up by the world. We want to be strong for our spouses, strong for our children, strong for our friends, and strong for our co-workers. However, we have to realize that our strength must be renewed, or we run the risk of wearing out before the bell.

My opponent in the ring lately has been *fear*. I read terrifying news stories, and my mind starts racing with a slew of "what-ifs." In no time at all I can work myself up into a state of silent panic. I find myself doing this more and more often as pictures of pure evil are daily filling my television screen, my cell phone alerts, and my Facebook newsfeed. The devil is hard at work and fear is one of his favorite tools. If he can make me feel afraid, he can weaken my faith; if my faith becomes weak, I can be easily knocked-out.

But I am *not* going to let him win. I choose faith.

My Coach stands ready with water and relief. He is able to restore my strength and reaffirm my hope. I don't even have to wait for the end of the round! I can go to Him in prayer at any moment, in any place, and fall at His feet in exhaustion. When I approach Him, He lifts me up, and reminds me that I am not just any fighter—I am His *child*—a child of the Most High God.

Feeling the strength building again within my soul, I rise to head back into the ring. As I turn to face fear again, I'm already swinging my fists and can hear the faith-building words of my Coach—my Heavenly Father—echoing all around me: *"Don't stop fighting...the end is near...and you have already won."*

STRENGTH

One of my favorite quotes of all time comes from the book *The Little Prince,* written by Antoine de Saint-Exupéry: "And now here is my secret, a very simple secret: It is only with the heart that one can see rightly; what is essential is invisible to the eye."

It reminds me of Hebrews 11:1, *"Now faith is the substance of things hoped for, the evidence of things not seen."* We don't know what life has in store. We don't even know what tomorrow will bring. We may experience things that we will never understand. We may be asked questions that we cannot answer. But, in the words of Paul, I KNOW whom I have believed! I am CONVINCED that he is keeping my life—my soul—which I have committed to him until the Day of Judgment.

Know what you believe and don't compromise!

> **What seen or unseen evidences exist in your life that contribute to your faith?** (Ask yourself this question: Why do I believe in God?)

How can you build up your faith so that it will support you in the good times as well as the difficult times?

TRIALS

Sometimes our faith is tested.

What can you do in those times to remain faithful? How do you keep on keeping on?

Sometimes God makes big changes in our lives through a series of small changes. We might not understand the little things that are happening, but they could be serving a greater purpose.

Martin Luther King Jr. once said "Faith is taking the first step even when you don't see the whole staircase."

Have you experienced this in your life? A moment you stepped out in faith, not knowing what would come next, but trusted in God as the builder of the staircase. How did it affect your faith?

Encouragement

"You are my God." These are the first four words found in Psalm 118:28, written by an unnamed author.

Try this exercise:
Say the phrase, "You are my God," out loud and emphasize the word "You."
Say it again and this time emphasize the word "are."
Again, say the phrase and emphasize the word "my."
Repeat it once more, emphasizing "God."

Each time you say the phrase, reflect on these comforting, faith-building truths:

YOU *are my God*: Unrivaled, unequaled, and unique. There is no other.
You **ARE** *my God*: Living, abiding, prevailing. Here and now.
You are **MY** *God*: Personal, special, individual. Belonging to me.
You are my **GOD**: Sovereign Lord, Creator, Master. My loving Shepherd and Heavenly Father.

Prayer

Almighty God, I praise you for the evidence of your presence all around me. I glorify you in the power you have shown us in your creation—from the mighty universe to the smallest cell. I am in awe of your greatness and am humbled that you are mindful of me.

Help me to trust you and to depend on you. Give me the courage to keep going when life is hard, when life is unfair and unforgiving. Help me to lean on you completely. Make my feet run to you in those times when all I want to do is run away.

I want to have a strong faith—a faith that keeps me going in the right direction; a faith that gets up when it's knocked down; a faith that keeps on keeping on. When I am tested, help me come though the fire praising, honoring, and glorifying Jesus Christ.

Thank you for the light of your Word that shows me the way to go.

In Jesus' Name, Amen

WALK WITH THE DOC

Walking tip: Walk for endurance

Could you walk 20-25 miles in a single day? Sounds like a monumental undertaking, yet that is what is referred to as a 'day's journey' in biblical times. Out of necessity, people of that period had considerable endurance when it came to walking. It was their primary means of travel. An excellent example of that endurance is found in Isaiah 40:31, "...they shall mount up with wings like eagles, they shall run and not be weary; they shall walk and not faint." We, too, are capable of building our endurance by establishing a walking program. Start by walking 30-40 minutes daily if possible. Over time extend the distance travelled in the same time period. That's all there is to it. A well-known Chinese proverb says: The journey of a thousand miles begins with a single step. If you're not already a walker, start today!

TAKE ACTION!

When it comes to exercise, do you mentally quit before you're physically ready? Sometimes your body might be saying, "I can do more!" while your brain is saying, "Nope, that's all I got!" Try to build on your current level of activity. You can do more than you think you can do!

Slowly push a *little* harder. Go a *little* farther. You'll see a difference in your endurance!

CHAPTER SEVEN
STAY OUT OF THE SHADOWS
Walk in the Light

"But if we walk in the light as He is in the light, we have fellowship with one another, and the blood of Jesus Christ His Son, cleanses us from all sin" (1 John 1:7).

I had no idea that the first year I spent at Short Mountain Bible Camp as a counselor would be a historic one. I was assigned to be with the older high school girls and looked forward to camp all summer. I love being around kids, but I really love those crazy, uncertain, ever-emotional teenagers! When I saw that my group had been placed in the "Locust cabin," I remained blissfully unaware of the dismal foreshadowing associated with a cabin named after an arthropod.

To say that the Locust cabin was primitive would be a titanic understatement. It was tucked right up next to the edge of the woods making it the perfect hideout for spiders, ticks, and other various specimens of the creepy-crawly nature. A mass of those "other various specimens" reared their ugly heads somewhere around the second day.

On Monday, heading back to the cabin after a morning of camp activities, I was eager to spend some quiet time on my bunk. When I walked in, right there, on the middle of the floor, was the biggest cricket I had ever seen. Huge back legs and super long antennae—it looked pretty ominous. I found out later that the official name for this particular type of bug is "cave cricket." At the time, I could not have cared less what it was called; I just wanted it out of my cabin!

Mission accomplished: cricket removed from the premises. But our troubles were just beginning. Upon closer inspection of the room, *there were others*. In fact, there were *many* others. They were clustered in corners, crawling up walls, and constantly clicking their little legs together. The Locust cabin had a certified cave cricket infestation!

An emergency action plan was initiated. All items were taken off the floor. The bunk beds were scooted to the middle of the room to form a double-decker island of safety. A roll of duct tape was obtained. And a quick trip to Dollar General secured us a collection of over-sized fly swatters— perfect for combatting cave crickets. It was on.

We realized that the crickets were coming from inside the walls of the cabin, so we used the duct tape to reinforce cracks and crevices. Each camper had her own swatter, we had a community dust pan, and we developed quite an effective strategy for insect detection and disposal. During daylight hours, we began to feel confident and capable of handling our insect intruders, but night time was a different story…

In the dark, the cave crickets were on the move. We could hear them chirping behind the walls assuring us they were there even if we couldn't see them, and we each had the constant threat of one jumping on us while we slept. It was maddening! We anxiously awaited morning, when the sun would bring light to every corner of the room, revealing the crickets, and giving us a fighting chance against their army!

The week ended, and we survived. We even made up a hysterical "cricket skit" to perform on the last night, complete with army face paint, camo, our over-sized fly swatters, and song lyrics that recounted the events of the week. Such an unforgettable experience!

Here is what the cave crickets taught me about light and darkness.

In the Light

There is no question that it was better when we could see. Plain and simple. When we could *see* the crickets (although they were ugly), it was better because we knew where they were, or we could find them. In the light of day, the girls and I could work as a team, pointing out crickets, saving each other from being jumped on, and coming up with ways to get them out of our cabin. In the light, we could even laugh and sing together as we battled the enemy!

The light exposed the truth! We had a cricket problem and there was no denying it as the light shone into even the darkest corners of the room. The light uncovered what we needed to know. It helped us to see what we were dealing with. It certainly didn't reveal a cabin of perfection; instead, it revealed a cabin that needed cleansing—of crickets!

Without the light, we would have been walking in and out of a darkened cabin with a cricket infestation, not aware of the reality. We may have become accustomed to stepping on them, feeling them land on us, hearing their incessant chirping, and as gross as that is, we may have eventually reached a point of indifference.

This is exactly what the Bible teaches us about light. The light is truth. In the light there is the promise of hope. There is joy. There is the confessing of sin. The light is perfect, but not so much the ones who are walking there. But they want to be. They try to be. They know that they will struggle with sin (or crickets), but they also know that being in the light is the only hope for salvation.

In the Dark

The dark brought fear. It brought uncertainty. We hid beneath our covers praying for the night to pass quickly. *Why?* Because we couldn't see! The darkness brought the terrible realization that we were not safe. We could not know where the crickets were hiding, or when they were moving, or if they were going to jump!

In the dark, it was "every man for himself." I couldn't even see the girls in the bunks next to me, and I was so busy worrying about the cricket bombers above my head that I'm not sure I could have been much help to anyone else. We tried to make ourselves feel better by saying things like, "The crickets are probably sleeping" or "Maybe the crickets go out at night." Of course neither of those was true, but that's what happens in the dark! Denial brings a false sense of comfort, and while you're busy tricking yourself into feeling better, something is sneaking up behind you!

Darkness hid our problem. It was there alright, but we couldn't see it. In the dark, we all suffered silently, shaking in our own sleeping bags, and fighting off our enemies alone. It was miserable. Hopeless.

The Bible teaches us that darkness brings with it the threat of despair. It's a place of misery. In the darkness there is denial of sin. It's ignored, so it *thrives*. There is no truth in the darkness; in fact, it is the complete absence of truth. If you live in darkness, you are living in a lie. You are in desperate need of saving.

You be the Light

She is a 'ministering angel' without any exaggeration in these hospitals, and as her slender form glides quietly along each corridor, every poor fellow's face softens with gratitude at the sight of her. When all the medical officers have retired for the night and silence and darkness have settled down upon those miles of prostrate sick, she may be observed alone, with a little lamp in her hand, making her solitary rounds.

Those words were printed in the British newspaper *The Times* in reference to Florence Nightingale, a woman remembered today as the founder of modern nursing. During the Crimean War she became known as "The Lady of the Lamp" because she would make her hospital rounds at night, carrying a small lantern and caring for wounded soldiers.

Florence Nightingale made it her mission in life to serve the hurting and the dying. She was not *of* the sick, but she was sent to work *in* hospitals *among* the sick to provide them with help and hope. She indeed was a "Lady of the Lamp:" *A light shining in the darkness.*

When Pilate questioned Jesus about the accusations brought against Him, Jesus answered by saying *"My kingdom is not of this world"* (John 18:36). Jesus was speaking about Heaven—the place of citizenship for the Christian (Philippians 3:20)—our focus, our hope, and our motivation while living on earth. In the book of James we read that our lives are *"a vapor, that appears for a little time and then vanishes away"* (James 4:14). Our time here is short, and we endure the pain, the suffering, and the trials, knowing that these "light afflictions" are momentary and are preparing an eternal glory for us to which nothing else can compare (2 Corinthians 4:17).

We are to be a separate people, knowing that we do not belong to this world or live according to its values. It is equally important to remember that we have been given a command to go *into* the world to preach the Gospel. As Florence Nightingale was sent into hospitals to care for the sick, we have been sent into the world to save the lost.

So here we are, in this world, with the divine charge not to be conformed to it (Romans 12:2), but also enlisted with the commission to go into the world and bring people to Jesus (Matthew 28:20).

Is it possible to go into the world and not be of the world?

It's what Jesus did.

It's what he prayed for his disciples, present and future.

Jesus recognized that his disciples, like him, are not of the world. In his prayer just before his arrest, Jesus did not ask God to take his disciples out of the world; rather, he asked that while they are here they may be kept from the "evil one" and be unified in him so that others may believe.

As a mother, I want to shield my children from the evils of this world. I want to protect their little hearts as long as I can. However, it is also my responsibility to teach my children how to live in this world as a Christian. I need to teach them how to be different *and* how to be approachable; how to resist temptation *and* how to shine in darkness; how to be separate *and* how to approach the lost—all at the same time. I have to prepare my children, and myself, to go into the world so we can bring others out of the world, while fighting the influences of the devil and remaining unified in Christ.

How do I do that? The answer is this: Through faithful study and application of God's Word. The Word is what makes us different; the Word is what transforms us; the Word is what separates us from the world. For us to go into the world but remain apart from the world, we must be fully armed for spiritual battle every day through our knowledge of and faithful obedience to the Word of God. We can either go into the world and be negatively influenced by it, or we can go into the world and be a positive influence to those around us by showing them the love of Christ through the Gospel message.

I want to be a "Lady of the Lamp." I want to be a light shining in the darkness. I want to be someone who brings hope to the hurting. I want to be close enough to the sick that they can see the light reflecting on my face and see the love of Christ. I want to be in situations where I can take a stand for what is right. I want the warmth and brightness of my lamp to draw people closer to God. I want to be recognized in the world by my light. I want to shine so that people know where to find me and be close enough for them to reach out and touch me. I want others to see me coming and know that I am someone who can offer help.

I imagine Florence Nightingale walking down a dark hall of the hospital with her lamp, caring for the sick lined up along the walls. I picture a wounded man at the end of hall watching the little flicker of light from her lamp and knowing that help was coming, yearning for the touch of the nurse. I pray that God will make me a "Lady of the Lamp" and that he will help me shine as I go out into this world and instill within me the sincere and loving desire to bring others out (*Trailblazers*, p. 194-196).

A WALKING WARRIOR

Nearly sixty years had passed since the death of Jesus, and the apostle John, now old in age, was living in Ephesus and continuing to minister to the church there. In around 90 A.D., after writing the fourth Gospel, John penned a series of letters that we know today as the Inspired books of 1, 2, and 3 John. The first letter was written to the churches of Asia Minor and centers on the theme of fellowship with God and with each other. It's fellowship that is characterized by walking in the light and walking in love. The third letter was written to a man named Gaius, who John is commending for his hospitality and for the support he has given "fellow workers for the truth." He also condemns a man named Diotrephes, a leader in the church who had become prideful and was acting in a way completely opposite of Gaius. Finally, there is the second letter of John, written to "the elect lady" about living and loving the truth. She is our walking in the light warrior! But who was she, who were her children, and what does she teach us today?

There is some debate over the identity of "the elect lady." Some people believe that she was an actual person, a faithful Christian woman and mother, who John knew personally. Others believe that "the elect lady" is simply a term of identification for the church and "her children" are the members. There are compelling arguments on each side. It's my personal belief that the latter is the most likely prospect, but regardless of the identity of the recipient, the message of John's letter is the same, and it's a message of great importance to Christians today!

John wrote to the elect lady on the subject of truth, which he tied tightly together with love. This is so beautifully expressed in John's letter and is a principle that is woven all throughout God's Word. Truth and love are friends; they are inseparable. There seems to be a misconception by some that in order to support the truth you can't have love, or in order to be loving you can't hold onto the truth. This is not what the Bible teaches. Truth and love work together; they complement each other. When we reach out to the world with the Truth of the Gospel and a sincere love for all people, we are following the example of Jesus and reflecting his very nature (John 14:6, 1 John 3:16).

In the first part of his letter, John wrote about the importance of practicing the truth and in the second part, the importance of protecting it. His letter is short in length, but long in wisdom. It's a message for the church as a whole and for each individual member. It's a message for you and me.

Practicing the Truth

In the greeting alone (vv. 1-3), John mentioned the word "truth" four times. This is an indication of what was on the heart of John as he sat down to write his letter. He began by telling the elect lady that he, along with all of those who have known the truth, love her in truth and because of the truth, which abides in them and lasts forever. He also told her that in truth and love the blessings of grace, mercy, and peace would be given to her by God the Father and his Son Jesus.

What is the truth? From John's words, we can determine that the truth is something you know, it's an expression of love, it lives inside of you, and it's eternal. The Bible tells us that the truth is God's Word (John 17:17). We can know it (John 8:32); we demonstrate love for each other and for God when we keep it (1 John 3:18, John 14:21-24); it dwells in us (Colossians 3:16), and it endures forever (1 Peter 1:25).

The Word, in its entirety, is truth. Truth is the definition of who Jesus is, the message of the Gospel, and the way in which God leads his children. If we want to know our Savior, if we want to know the hope of Heaven that he gave us through his life, death, and resurrection, and if we want to know what God expects from us, we will find what we are seeking in the trustworthy and never-changing Word of Truth.

In the next three verses, John praised the lady after hearing that her children were walking in the truth. This is why she was chosen as our warrior! Truth is light and light is truth. They carry the same meaning. To walk in truth is to walk in the light. In his previous letter, John said it like this: "to walk in darkness is not to practice the truth" (1 John 1:6), and in the book of John he quoted these words of Jesus: "he who does the truth comes to the light" (John 3:21). The elect lady and her children were living in the truth, and because they were living in the truth, they were also living in the light.

Building on this, John pleaded with the reader that "we love one another." In verses five and six, John defined love as walking according to his commandments. Here the truth-love bond is realized! Love is living a life of faithful obedience to the truth! You can't have one without the other. When you practice the truth, you're practicing love, and when you practice love, you're practicing the truth. This has been God's expectation from the beginning.

Protecting the Truth

John's letter also came with a warning. He wanted his readers to be aware of the danger of false teachers in the world who were denying that Jesus had come in the flesh. John referred to them as "deceivers" and "anti-christs." This was the reason he wanted his readers to be attentive to walking in truth and love every day. In doing that, they would remain strong and stand ready when confronted by those false teachers. He earnestly charged them saying, "Watch yourselves! Don't lose what you've worked for so that you can receive a full reward!"

In verse nine, John emphasized the importance of doctrine. He stated that whoever goes beyond the doctrine of Christ, or doesn't abide in it, does not have God. When we make up our own rules, or when we fail to keep the commandments that God has given us in his Word, we lose our relationship with him. Some people feel that what each of us believes individually doesn't really matter, but that is not what we are told by the Holy Spirit in 2 John 9. Doctrine matters! It matters to the point of having God or not having God.

John instructed that if anyone came bringing a different doctrine, he was not to be welcomed into the house or even greeted. If "elect lady" is a reference to the church, then "house" would be a reference to the place of worship. Either way, a false teacher should not be encouraged or supported in order to avoid being guilty of taking part in his evil work.

The letter John wrote to the elect lady is a picture of what it means to walk in the light. It's living a life based on truth and grounded in love. It's avoiding darkness and those who attempt to extinguish light. Individually, our lives should be testimonies to truth and love. Together, as the church, we are the pillar and ground of the truth (1 Timothy 3:15), and the world will know us to be disciples of Christ by our love (John 13:35). We are the light of the world. It is our responsibility to shine so that God can be glorified.

IN HIS STEPS

"Then Jesus spoke to them again, saying, 'I am the _____ of the _____. He who follows Me shall not walk in _____, but have the _____ of _____'" (John 8:12).

"I have come as a _____ into the world, that whoever believes in Me should not abide in _____" (John 12:46).

Jesus IS the light of the world (John 8:12). If we abide in him, we will not abide in darkness (John 12:46).

OUR DAILY WALK _____

One morning on one of the first days of December a couple of years back, Briggs brought me a letter that he had written to Santa Claus.

"Are you letting Santa know what you want for Christmas?" I asked him.
"No, not yet," he answered, "First, I need to find out which list I'm on."

Briggs had been wondering whether his name was written on the naughty list or the nice list; and before bothering to write out a wish list, he needed to be sure about where he stood with Santa! As Christians, when it comes to our daily walk, we don't have to wonder whether we are walking in the light or walking in the dark. We can know for a fact! If we love God, love the Truth, and are faithfully trying to live in obedience to God's Word, then we are walking in the light. If we are distancing ourselves from God, not practicing the Truth, and not trying to follow God's Word, then we are walking in darkness.

Remember the story of Eutychus? (Acts 20:7-12). He was the young man who fell asleep while he was sitting in a window listening to Paul preach. He tumbled out into the darkness from three stories above the ground and was found dead. Paul fell on top of him, embraced him, and Eutychus' life was restored. There are a few things to learn from this story that can help us in our daily walking.

First, notice in verses 7-8 that it was midnight and that "there were many lamps in the upper room where they were gathered." The room was filled with light, but Eutychus sat in a window that bumped right up to the darkness. Next, he got comfortable. Then, he fell. His fall landed him in complete darkness, and he lost his life. Thankfully, Paul was there to help. He revived Eutychus and brought him back into the well-lit house where he was fed and everyone was encouraged.

To be sure that you are daily walking in the light, ask yourself these questions:

Where have you chosen to sit?
Have you become too comfortable there?
Are you in danger of falling?

If you've already fallen, the good news is that you can come back to light! There are people who want to restore you, embrace you, feed you, and comfort you.

STRENGTH

When it comes to the light, we walk with purpose and direction, not perfection. Our desire is for God and not for the world, and we rely on the Truth to guide our lives.

How can we grow in our understanding of the Truth?

What are some of the joys and blessings that come with walking in the light?

How are you shining the light of the Truth in the world?

TRIALS

Are there challenges that come with walking in the light? If so, what are they?

Darkness is tempting because we can hide our sins there. Walking in the light involves honesty and confession. What does 1 John 1:9 say will happen if we confess our sins?

We live in a world that would like you to think that Truth doesn't really matter. How are we practicing the Truth and in what ways are we protecting it?

Read 2 Corinthians 11:13-15. What does it mean that Satan is an angel of light?

ENCOURAGEMENT

Find a quiet place, at a quiet time, to spend in quiet devotion reading Scriptures that refer to "light." I am going to suggest something a little different, but I believe that you will find it meaningful: read these Bible verses in the dark, by candlelight. If you don't have a candle, you can use a flashlight—or even the light of your cellphone. Turn off all of the lights, except for the one that you are using to read. Whisper the words of the Bible verses quietly and meditate on their teaching. Think about the light *you* are shining through your life. Thank God for bringing you out of the darkness.

Here is a list of "light" Scriptures for your reference:

Psalm 27:1
Psalm 119:105, 130
Matthew 5:14-16
John 1:1-9
John 8:1-12
John 12:35-36
Ephesians 5:8-14
James 1:17-18
1 Peter 2:9-10
1 John 1:5-9
Revelation 21:22-27

PRAYER

You are the Father of Lights with whom there is no variation or shifting shadow. Help me to walk as a child of light. Keep me from the darkness. Protect me under your wing where I will be safe from evil.

I thank you for your Word of Truth that will stand forever. Through it, I pray that you will show me what is acceptable to you. Direct my steps so that I will remain in the light far from the edge of darkness.

I humbly bow before you in gratitude for the blood of Jesus Christ that continually washes away my sin. Provide me with the courage I need to be honest and to confess my faults so that I can be cleansed from unrighteousness.

In Jesus' Name, Amen

WALK WITH THE DOC

Walking tip: Walk with Intelligence

Knowledge is defined as information, understanding, or skill that you can get from experience or education. Intelligence is defined as the ability to apply knowledge. Many suffer, or even perish, due to lack of knowledge about health and wellness, or having gained that knowledge, lack the intelligence to effectively apply it. The following guidelines are based upon solid science and should be added to your knowledge base and applied intelligently to stay on the road to wellness: minimize the stress in your life; engage in regular exercise; avoid tobacco, recreational drugs, and alcohol; achieve a healthy weight and maintain it; pursue an active lifestyle; and eat a healthy diet. Think young! Engage your brain, be a student for life, stay close to friends and family, get adequate rest, and stay positive. Be wise, persevere, and be healthy!

TAKE ACTION!

Knowledge is power! It's important to be educated when it comes to your physical body. What diseases run in your family? What medical conditions are you currently experiencing? Do your research on disease prevention, managing symptoms, diet and exercise recommendations, early warning signs of various illnesses, and more! Know where to go for good, reliable, updated information. As a general rule, websites sponsored by the U.S. government, not-for-profit health or medical organizations, and university medical centers are considered reliable resources for information.

Take some time to look through some of these on-line resources for health and wellness:

ACE Fitness
Alzheimer's Association
American Cancer Society
American Diabetes Association
American Heart Association
Choose My Plate (USDA)
LIVESTRONG
Mayo Clinic
MedlinePlus

CHAPTER EIGHT

FOLLOW YOUR GUIDE

Walk by the Spirit

"I say then: Walk in the Spirit, and you shall not fulfill the lust of the flesh" (Galatians 5:16).

Our family loves to travel! We get excited about road trips and all of the fun that comes with planning where we'll stay, where we'll eat, and the "touristy" things we'll do. We make lists of everything we would like to experience (well, okay...*I* actually make the lists, but I'm always open to suggestions...as long as they fit in the schedule...on the right day...and in the appropriate time slot), and we countdown to the day of departure.

One Spring Break we decided to spend the week in Savannah, Georgia. We had never been there before and were looking forward to a fantastic visit! We packed up the Expedition (as we've done so many times before) and drove the nearly seven hours toward the eastern coast of Georgia. It was a great trip, with all of the usual craziness that I wouldn't trade for anything.

We all fell in love with Savannah! The history, the architecture, the flowers, the food—we could have spent many more days soaking up the essence of that beautiful city! The only problem we had was with the weather. It rained almost every day we were there. But, no worries! I was thrilled to find a shop along River Street that sold ponchos, and I bought one for each of us! (The kids did *not* share in my enthusiasm).

At one point we were standing on a street corner, in the rain, feeling lost and trying to figure out where we needed to go. We all had on our big yellow ponchos, and I was holding up a gigantic unfolded map of the city with a Canon camera hanging around my neck. As we were all turning circles, glancing every which way, looking up addresses on our phones, one of our kids declared, "This is SO embarrassing. We totally look like tourists."

And we did. We looked like a visiting family of confused over-sized ducks. Confused ducks with maps, cameras, and cellphones. It was quite a sight, I'm sure.

I explained to the kids, "Of course we look like tourists! That's what we are!" We didn't look or act like the people from there, because we're *not* from there. Savannah was a pretty place, and we had some memorable times there, but it wasn't our home. As much as we enjoyed it, everything we did while we were there was done with the understanding that we would be heading home soon.

So it is with children of God. We're pilgrims in this world. Sojourners. We should stick out as people who don't belong here. We live with a different focus, a different standard, a different hope. When the world looks at us, they should see over-sized ducks, with maps, cameras, and cellphones! (Not really). But they should recognize us as people who are not from here; people who are traveling. To the world we should look like *tourists*—a people who are traveling home.

Walking by the Spirit means not walking by the flesh. It involves living a life that is not according to fleshly desires. When others look at us, they should see people who are living in a way that is unlike the world. They should see *spiritually* minded people (Romans 8:1-11).

How we live our lives depends on where we've set our minds, or on those things with which we fill our minds. Are we setting our minds on fleshly things, or are we setting our minds on spiritual things? Colossians 3:2 says, *"If then you were raised with Christ seek those things which are above, where Christ is, sitting at the right hand of God. Set your mind on things above, not on things on the earth."*

What do we have to do in order to become spiritually minded people? What does it take to live according to the Spirit? First, we have to allow ourselves to be born of the Spirit, so that we might begin a new life in obedience to the Word. Next, we have to allow ourselves to be fed by the Spirit, so that our minds will be filled with the Word. Then, we have to allow ourselves to be led by the Spirit, so that our feet can be guided by the Word.

When we are born of the Spirit, fed by him, and led by him, our walk to the Promised Land will be spiritually focused and fruit-filled—all by the means of God's Word.

Spirit Bred

In John 4, we read about the conversation Jesus had at night with Nicodemus, a Pharisee and ruler of the Jews. Jesus explained to him that a man had to be born again in order to see the kingdom of God. Nicodemus asked the question, *"How can a man be born when he is old? Can he enter a second time into his mother's womb and be born?"*

Jesus answered, *"Most assuredly, I say to you, unless one is born of water and the Spirit, he cannot enter the kingdom of God. That which is born of the flesh is flesh, and that which is born of the Spirit is spirit."*

How can someone be born of the water and the Spirit? Our rebirth occurs through baptism by the means of the Word. In Ephesians 5:25-26, we read, *"Husbands love your wives, just as Christ also loved the church and gave Himself for her that He might sanctify and cleanse her with the washing of water by the word."* The Word of God is the sword of the Spirit (Ephesians 6:17). It's the instrument that is used by the Spirit in order to convict the hearts of people. It's what happened to the men and women on the Day of Pentecost when they heard the truth spoken by Peter. They were cut to their hearts! Convicted! That conviction led them to respond in faithful obedience through repentance and baptism; thus they were born again of water and the Spirit.

In Titus 3:4-7, Paul describes the rebirth through which God saves us, saying: *"But when the kindness and the love of God our Savior toward man appeared, not by works of righteousness which we have done, but according to His mercy, He saved us, through the washing of regeneration and renewing of the Holy Spirit, whom He poured out on us abundantly through Jesus Christ our Savior, that having been justified by His grace we should become heirs according to the hope of eternal life."*

We obey the truth and are born again through the Word of God, the instrument of the Spirit, which lives forever (1 Peter 1:22-23). We are also born again in a watery grave of baptism so that our sins can be removed by the blood of Jesus Christ, and we can rise up out of the water a new person, living a new life. Paul wrote to the Romans about baptism in Romans 6:3-4, *"Or do you not know that as many of us as were baptized into Christ Jesus were baptized into His death? Therefore, we were buried with Him through baptism into death, that just as Christ was raised from the dead by the glory of the Father, even so we also should walk in newness of life."*

We are born of the Spirit through the Word.

Spirit Fed

A desperate father fell at the feet of Jesus. His twelve-year-old daughter—his only child—lay dying in her bed at their home. In agony, knowing she had little time left, he begged for Jesus to come and make her well.

As Jesus went, the crowds were pushed so closely around him that it was difficult for him to move. I imagine the father of the sick girl trying to clear the way, calling out "Let the Teacher through!" thinking of his precious daughter and urgently working to get Jesus to her side. Then, someone came from his house and told him not to trouble Jesus any longer. It was too late—his daughter had died.

But death does not stop Jesus.

He continued on to the house of the grieving father, where people had already gathered to mourn the death of his child. Jesus went to her room, stood at her bedside, took her hand, and said "Little girl, arise!" and she arose immediately.

What I find especially interesting is what Jesus said to her parents right after he restored their child's life: *"Give her something to eat."*

He had just performed a miracle! He had defied the impossible! He had taken what was lifeless and made it alive again and his first words were *"Feed her!"*

Throughout his ministry Jesus recognized the physical need for food and drink; not only for his followers, but also for himself.

- He miraculously fed thousands of people who had gathered to hear him speak all day, using only five loaves of bread and two fish, because he was concerned about their hunger.
- On the cross, in physical and emotional pain, Jesus called out, "I thirst!"
- When he appeared to his disciples after his resurrection, Jesus showed them his hands and his feet and told them to feel his flesh and bones to convince them that he was alive again! As they stood there in disbelief mixed with joy, Jesus asked, "Have you any food here?" Then, he ate with them.

Jesus understood hunger, and he understood thirst. He *felt* them just as we do. I find it remarkable that he has taken our physical need for nourishment—something tangible, something we can *feel*—and he related it to our spiritual need for nourishment.

He tells us that he is the Bread of Life (John 6:35).
He refers to himself as the Giver of Living Water (John 4:10).
He calls us to hunger and thirst for righteousness (Matthew 5:6).
He wants us to feed on the milk and meat of the Word, to taste the good Word of God, and to be nourished with faith and sound doctrine—as we read in the biblical letters of inspired men (Hebrews 5:12; 1 Corinthians 3:2).

Physical hunger must be satisfied, and the same is true with spiritual hunger. One comes from food and drink, while the other comes from Jesus Christ and the Spirit through the Word of God. Strength, growth, and renewal are necessary for our bodies and for our souls, every single day. Even after we have died to our sins in baptism and been raised to walk a new life—just as he commanded the resurrected daughter of Jairus—Jesus says *"Eat!"*

We are fed by the Spirit through the Word.

Spirit Led

We are led by the Spirit of God. Romans 8:14 says, *"For as many as are led by the Spirit of God, these are sons of God."* The question is not, *does* he lead us, but rather, *how* does the Spirit lead us? He leads us using the same instrument he uses to feed us and convict us: the perfect and eternal Word of God.

"knowing this first, that no prophecy of Scripture is of any private interpreta-

tion, for prophecy never came by the will of man, but holy men of God spoke as they were moved by the Holy Spirit" (2 Peter 1:20-21).

The Word was delivered by the Spirit, confirmed by him, and is used by him today to change the hearts and minds of mankind. We are led by the Spirit through the Word in a variety of ways. Here is a collection of Bible verses that describe his leadership:

THE SPIRIT TEACHES US THROUGH THE WORD: *"These things we also speak, not in words which man's wisdom teaches but which the Holy Spirit teaches, comparing spiritual things with spiritual"* (1 Corinthians 2:13).

THE SPIRIT REVEALS THE NATURE OF GOD THROUGH THE WORD: *"Of this salvation the prophets have inquired and searched carefully, who prophesied of the grace that would come to you, searching what, or what manner of time, the Spirit of Christ who was in them was indicating when He testified beforehand the sufferings of Christ and the glories that would follow. To them it was revealed that, not to themselves, but to us they were ministering the things which now have been reported to you through those who have preached the gospel to you by the Holy Spirit sent from Heaven—things which angels desire to look into"* (1 Peter 1:10-12).

THE SPIRIT GUIDES US INTO ALL TRUTH: *"However, when He, the Spirit of truth, has come, He will guide you into all truth; for He will not speak on His own authority, but whatever He hears he will speak; and He will tell you things to come"* (John 16:13; John 17:17 – The Word is truth).

THE SPIRIT PROVIDES US WITH TEACHING, REPROOF, CORRECTION, AND TRAINING THROUGH THE WORD: *"All Scripture is given by inspiration of God, and is profitable for doctrine, for reproof, for correction, for instruction in righteousness"* (2 Timothy 3:16).

THE SPIRIT SHOWS US WHERE TO GO THROUGH THE WORD: *"Your word is a lamp unto my feet and a light to my path"* (Psalm 119:105).

THE SPIRIT COMFORTS US THROUGH THE WORD: *"Remember the word to Your servant, upon which You have caused me to hope. This is my comfort in my affliction, for Your word has given me life"* (Psalm 119:49-50).

THE SPIRIT STRENGTHENS US THROUGH THE WORD: *"So now, brethren, I commend you to God and to the word of His grace, which is able to build you up and give you an inheritance among all those who are sanctified"* (Acts 20:32).

We are led by the Spirit through the Word.

A Fruitful Harvest

When we have been born of the water and the Spirit, and we continue to allow ourselves to be fed and led by the Spirit, then his fruit will be produced in our lives! In Galatians 5:22-23, Paul describes the fruit of the Spirit as: *love, joy, peace, patience, kindness, goodness, faithfulness, gentleness, and self-control.*

This fruit will become evident in the lives of people who study the Word and follow its instruction and teaching in their daily lives. They love the Word and treat it respectfully. They allow it to be planted in their heart and become deeply rooted as they grow stronger and stronger in the faith. They learn from both the Old and New Testaments. They hear the truth, and it changes them; they don't walk away from a message from the Word unaffected. They delight in Bible study. They look to Scripture for advice, for comfort, and for direction. They share the Word with others. They obey it. They see the big picture of God's eternal plan from the words, "In the beginning" to the final "Amen." They see God's grace on every page of the Bible.

A wonderful thing happens to these people. They become more loving, more joyful, more peaceful, more patient, more kind and good, more faithful, more gentle, and more self-controlled. Their lives spill over with this beautiful fruit! These people are truly "Spirit filled," not in a miraculous sense, but simply because they have filled themselves up with the imperishable, life-giving, freedom-making, separating, power-wielding, salvation-bearing Word of God.

We bear the fruit of the Spirit when we apply the Word to our lives.

A powerful image comes to my mind when I think of this walking warrior. I picture a man, barely standing, his body battered from the stones that have been thrown at him over and over again. He is bruised and bloody and death is very near. I imagine his head turned toward the sky, but instead of fear or pain, there is complete joy reflected on his face because he sees something that no one else can. Looking up, he sees the heavens opened and Jesus standing at the right hand of God! He calls out, *"Lord Jesus, receive my spirit."* In my mind he falls to his knees, with his arms lifted upward, and loudly cries, *"Lord, do not charge them with this sin."* Then he closes his eyes, an expression of peace covers his face, he gently lowers himself to the ground, and he gives his soul to God.

The disciple known as Stephen was the first Christian martyr, a man of godly character, and a courageous witness who didn't fear death. We can learn many things from this spirit-filled follower of Christ. His story is found in the sixth and seventh chapters of Acts.

The first mention of Stephen is found in Acts 6:5 where he is described as "a man full of faith and the Holy Spirit." In the preceding verses, attention had been brought to the fact that the Hellenists' widows were being neglected when it came to receiving a portion of the daily distribution of money collected by the church under the oversight of the apostles. Stephen had been one of seven men chosen by the disciples to assume the responsibility of apportioning the funds collected for those in need. Those seven men where characterized collectively as being "men of good reputation, full of the Holy Spirit and wisdom."

Stephen's story continues in verse 8 as the stage is being set for the first Christian to die for his faith. *"And Stephen, full of faith* (NASB, *grace) and power, did great wonders and signs among the people. Then there arose some from what is called the Synagogue of the Freedmen (Cyrenians, Alexandrians, and those from Cilicia and Asia), disputing with Stephen. And they were not able to resist the wisdom and the Spirit by which he spoke."*

So they plotted against Stephen, stirred up the people, and falsely accused him of blasphemy against Moses and God. He was seized and brought before the Jewish council with this condemnation: *"This man does not cease to speak blasphemous words against this holy place and the law; for we have heard him say that this Jesus of Nazareth will destroy this place and change the customs which Moses delivered to us."* The high priest stood before Stephen and addressed him with the question, *"Are these things so?"*

What follows in the seventh chapter of Acts is a powerful sermon given by Stephen that both shocked and angered his accusers. He boldly recounted the sinful history of the Israelite nation as time after time they rejected God, and in the end he denounced them for the betrayal and murder of the Messiah. Stephen preached that God "does not dwell in a temple made with hands" and indicated that people anywhere on the earth can find God and worship him. Stephen's accusers would hear no more. The council had become enraged—to the point of murder.

Then comes the powerful image of a Spirit-filled warrior who courageously faced death in a way that is reminiscent of Jesus' final hours.

Stephen was described as being "full of the Holy Spirit," and his life was characterized by wisdom, faith, grace, and power. While he received the Spirit in a miraculous sense, enabling him to perform wonders and signs, we can possess the same virtues when we fill our lives with the Word of God, the means by which the Spirit works today.

Wisdom

Stephen was known among his fellow disciples as being a man of wisdom. It's one of the reasons they chose him to serve as a leader in the church. I believe he possessed what is described in James 3:17 as *"the wisdom that is from above,"* which is *"first pure, then peaceable, gentle, willing to yield, full of mercy and good fruits, without partiality and without hypocrisy."* His wisdom can be seen in the way he uses his knowledge of Jewish history to challenge the council members with the truth. He is bold, but for the sake of peace. He is outspoken, but for the sake of unity.

Today, the Spirit works in our lives to make us wise through the Word. In 2 Timothy 3:15, Paul wrote to Timothy about continuing in the things he had learned including his knowledge of the Holy Scriptures, which Paul said "are able to make you wise for salvation through faith which is in Christ Jesus." Continuing on in that text, verses 16-17 tell us that all Scripture, which is breathed from the mouth of God, is useful for teaching, convincing, correcting, and training for righteousness, and thoroughly equips us for every good work. By studying the Word, we grow in understanding; by living the Word we grow in wisdom.

We become wise through the knowledge and application of the Word by the work of the Spirit. This is the wisdom that is from above. This is the wisdom that will help us bear the fruit of the Spirit. This is the wisdom that filled Stephen.

Faith

Stephen was faithful. He believed in Jesus Christ, he hoped for a home in Heaven, and he was obedient to the Gospel. We know this because he was counted among the disciples in the early church and was specifically recognized in Scripture as being a man of full of faith. He is among those nameless heroes mentioned in the great faith chapter, Hebrews 11, who suffered persecution and of whom the world was not worthy.

We can see the faith of Stephen in just the small glimpse we are given into his life. It's by faith he became a Christian, by faith he served the church, by faith he performed miracles, by faith he spoke the Truth, by faith he testified before the high priest and Jewish council, by faith he defended Christ, by faith he convicted his accusers, and by faith he bravely gave his life for the purpose of the Gospel.

Today, our faith comes through hearing the Word (Hebrews 10:17), which has been given to us by the Spirit (2 Peter 1:19-21). The Word of God is the weapon our Lord has given us to fight our spiritual battles; and the more we use it, the stronger our faith will become. I pray to have the faith of Stephen.

Grace

Stephen is also described as being full of grace. He seemed to have an understanding of the mystery of the Gospel: that all people could be heirs to God's promises in Christ; and had the council not become so violently angry, he might have preached about the gift of God's grace to Jews and Gentiles alike through the death of Jesus.

I see Stephen in the words that Paul spoke to the Ephesian elders in Acts

20:22-24. *"And see, now I go bound in the spirit to Jerusalem, not knowing the things that will happen to me there, except that the Holy Spirit testifies in every city, saying that chains and tribulations await me. But none of these things move me; nor do I count my life dear to myself, so that I may finish my race with joy, and the ministry which I received from the Lord Jesus, to testify to the gospel of the grace of God."*

The ministry of Stephen did not last as long as the ministry of Paul in a physical sense, but his testimony to the Gospel of Grace is remembered forever in Scripture. He took a strong stand. He died courageously and compassionately. In the end, the church grew because of his effort for the cause of Christ.

Today, we hold within ourselves the treasure of the Gospel (2 Corinthians 4:7), and we are called to be stewards of that treasure. Through the Word, the Spirit has placed in our hands the Gospel of Grace, and it is our responsibility to share it with others. Understanding that God desires for all men to be saved, and having in our possession the means to teach others about the same grace that gives us hope, should inspire us to "Go into all the world..."

Power

The miraculous power of the Holy Spirit allowed Stephen to perform great wonders and signs. Then, at the end of his life, the power of the Spirit helped him to fearlessly face death. Stephen submitted to the Spirit, and the Spirit filled him with power. Is it possible for us to receive power through the Spirit today?

Yes, we can still experience the power of the Spirit, but not in all of the same ways that Stephen experienced it. Now that we have the complete, revealed Word of God, there is no longer a need for miraculous wonders and signs. Today our power comes through knowledge of the Gospel given to us by the Spirit. Romans 1:16 says, *"For I am not ashamed of the gospel of Christ for it is the power of God to salvation for everyone who believes for the Jew first and also for the Greek."*

It is also by the power of the Spirit that we are made free from the law of sin and death! Because we died to our old selves in baptism and now walk a new life in Christ being led by the Spirit, we will suffer no condemnation

(Romans 8:1-4)! We don't have to fear death, just as Stephen didn't fear death. When our time comes, we can joyfully speak the words of Paul in 2 Corinthians 5:8, *"We are confident, yes, well pleased rather to be absent from the body and to be present with the Lord."*

The Holy Spirit empowers us today through the Word. If we read it, study it, meditate on it, and apply it, he will work mightily in our lives.

IN HIS STEPS

By the power of the Spirit, Jesus was led (Matthew 4:1), anointed (Luke 4:18-19), taught (Isaiah 11:2), given the words of God to speak (John 3:34), and raised from the dead (Romans 8:11). Through the Spirit, Jesus fulfilled his eternal purpose and accomplished the will of the Father. Jesus walked by the Spirit in perfect obedience and without sin.

"For if the blood of _____ and _____ and the ashes of a heifer, sprinkling the unclean, sanctifies for the purifying of the flesh, how much more shall the _____ of _____, who through the eternal _____ offered Himself without _____ to God, cleanse your conscience from dead works to serve the living _____" (Hebrews 9:14).

OUR DAILY WALK

If we are going to walk by the Spirit, we have to let go of the flesh. Remember that you are a child of God with a great future; a future that doesn't rest in the confines of this physical place. We have our hearts set on another life, in a heavenly country, where there is a city that has been prepared for us by God (Hebrews 11:16)! How we live now, in this place, determines where we'll be then, when the gates of that city are opened.

Keeping that in mind, *daily*, is important. It's not always easy, but there are some things we can do to remind ourselves that we are pilgrims, and this world is not our home. The first thing we can do is really look at ourselves and decide whether we are living for spiritual things or for worldly things. Are we spiritually focused, or are we focused on the here-and-now desires of the flesh? What is the condition of our inner man? Are we becoming spiritually stronger every day?

Once you've examined yourself, allow the Spirit to work in your life through his Holy Word. Allow him to feed you and lead you as you study the Bible and then live out his teaching as you walk day to day. Renew your mind continually with the only thing we have in this world that is not of this world—the God-breathed Word! Meditate on Scripture, let it penetrate your heart, guide your life, and transform you more and more into the image of Christ. *That's* the power of the Spirit!

Be careful to invest as much time in your inner-self as you do for your outer-self. Don't neglect your spiritual health and spiritual growth. Set aside time every day to strengthen the part of you that is going to live forever! The Spirit will help you by using the most powerful tool available for our training—the Word of God. Read and study it! Live and share it!

Then, prepare to open up a fruit stand because there will be a harvest! The Spirit will bear his fruit in your life abundantly. When you are born again by the water and the Spirit by the power of the Word, then feed on the Word, and are led by the Word, the evidence of the Spirit's work in your life will be unmistakable.

STRENGTH

Imagine two people: one is walking by the Spirit, the other by the flesh. Consider the characteristics of each of their lives. How are they different?

What are the results that come from having a strong inner man?

Do you know someone who you can tell obviously "walks by the Spirit?" What is it about him or her that makes it evident?

TRIALS

What does the devil try to do to keep us from walking by the Spirit?

The devil doesn't play fair. He wants us to live by the flesh, and he uses our weaknesses to try to keep us bound to the world. In what ways does he tempt you the most on your daily walk?

How does walking with a spiritual focus help us in times of difficulty or trial?

ENCOURAGEMENT

Saying "no" to the flesh and "yes" to the Spirit is key to Kingdom living. When we are fed by the Spirit and led by the Spirit, we will see fruitful results. What do those results look like in our everyday lives? The virtuous products of a life that is lived according to the Spirit are found in Galatians 5:22-23. Think about the fruit of the Spirit and how these Godly characteristics can be seen in your life, or how you would like for it to be seen. Write down some specific examples:

Love –

Joy –

Peace –

Patience –

Kindness –

Goodness –

Faithfulness –

Gentleness –

Self-Control –

PRAYER

Create in me a clean heart O God, and renew a steadfast spirit within me. Do not cast me from your presence, and do not take your Holy Spirit from me.

Restore to me the joy of your salvation, and uphold me by your generous Spirit. Then I will teach transgressors your ways, and sinners shall be converted to you (Psalm 51:10-13).

Lead me by your Truth. Fill my heart with your Word. Help my life to bear the fruit of the Spirit.

I pray for wisdom, courage, and grace. When my time in this world has come to an end, please receive my spirit.

In Jesus' Name, Amen

WALK WITH THE DOC

Walking tip: Walk for your heart

Heart disease is a leading cause of death in the United States; and given the rising rates of obesity and diabetes in this country, it will remain so well into the future. Exercise is a key factor in reducing the risk of heart disease. All forms of exercise are good, but especially those that get the heart rate up. Walking is an excellent form of exercise, but it is recommended that it be brisk in nature. The heart is a muscle, and when it is exercised it gets stronger, improving blood supply to the heart and brain. Exercise, in combination with a healthy diet, is essential in dealing with this nation's epidemic of obesity. Walking is, and will remain, a major weapon in the fight against heart disease.

TAKE ACTION!

It's a good idea to regularly monitor your heart rate, rhythm, and blood pressure. This is especially important as you age, and if you are actively involved in an exercise program. In fact, it's a good idea to know all of your "numbers:" cholesterol, tri-glycerides, blood cell counts, thyroid, liver function, etc. If you've never had baseline lab work done, or if it's been a long time, you might want to consider visiting your doctor so you will know where you stand.

One thing you can start doing right away is monitor your heart rate and rhythm before and after walking. Your heart rate, or pulse, is the number of times your heart beats each minute. A normal resting heart rate ranges from 60 – 100 beats. To check your pulse at your wrist, place two fingers between the bone and the tendon over your radial artery — which is located on the thumb side of your wrist.

When you feel your pulse, count the number of beats over 60 seconds. During exercise try to stay between 50 percent to 85 percent of your maximum heart rate (MHR). The MHR (roughly calculated as 220 minus your age) is the upper limit of what your cardiovascular system can handle during physical activity.

CHAPTER NINE

WALK TALL

Walk Uprightly

"For the Lord God is a sun and shield; The Lord will give grace and glory; no good thing will He withhold from those who walk uprightly" (Psalm 84:11).

*T*hose precious first steps. The excitement! The smiles! The pictures! Wobbly legs awkwardly moving and outstretched arms eagerly grasping for a prize that is just out of reach. One step...and cheers! Another step...and more cheers! And another...until the child falls into the embrace of an enthusiastic fan! It's a milestone. A day that calls for a quiet reading of *If I Could Keep You Little* and, for this mom, an equitable mix of happy and sad tears.

Briggs, our youngest child, began walking at an early age, probably in an attempt to keep up with his two older, louder, and busier sisters. Sometimes, when he ran out of patience waiting on his legs to get him where he wanted to go, he would crawl over to the little kids' table in our kitchen and pull himself up into a standing position using one of the chairs for support. Then, he would place his hands on the seat of the chair and use it like a walker, pushing it everywhere with his feet shuffling behind. He could maneuver that chair in and out of rooms and around corners at hypersonic speed! It was the cutest, and occasionally the scariest, thing.

Babies who are just learning to take their first steps can teach us important lessons on living uprightly. The word "upright" means honest and righteous. In the Bible, it's associated with blamelessness and is pleasing to God (Job 1:8). How does one become an upright person? This is where the walking babies come in and provide some tender-footed instruction.

Have a Heart

A person who lives uprightly is a person whose heart yearns for God. Think of that baby, carefully walking toward a mother or father who is crouched down with wide open arms whispering words of encouragement and strength. *"You can do it! That's it! Just one more step!"* The baby's eyes are set on the goal; his heart already rests in the arms of his mom or dad; he just has to get his feet there. Sometimes those legs begin to move faster as he gets closer and those sweet baby grunts get louder as the anticipation grows!

How passionate are we about walking toward our Father? Are we reaching out to him with our heart and soul? Do we truly want to be with him? When I think about someone who desired God completely and authentically, I think about David.

Listen to the words of these psalms:

"My soul longs, yes, even faints for the courts of the Lord; my heart and my flesh cry out for the living God" (Psalm 84:2).

"O God, You are my God; early will I seek You; my soul thirsts for You; my flesh longs for You in a dry and thirsty land where there is no water" (Psalm 63:1).

"As the deer pants for the water brooks, so pants my soul for You, O God. My soul thirsts for God, for the living God. When shall I come and appear before God?" (Psalm 42:1-2).

Does your heart cry out for God? Does your flesh long for him? Does your soul thirst for him?

Psalm 11:7 says, *"For the Lord is righteous, He loves righteousness; His countenance beholds the upright."* Scholars debate about whether this means "the Lord will see the upright" or "the upright will see God." Either way, both are true! God watches over his people, providentially, with affection and grace (Numbers 6:24-26), and men are to seek God through purity and righteousness (Psalm 17:15, Matthew 5:8).

An upright person desires to be in the presence of God and wants to see his face, and God stands in front of her with arms spread offering blessings and peace. Our steps may be shaky, and it may be hard to move at times, but are we reaching out and trying to get there? God is holding open his arms and whispering those words of encouragement and strength to you and me. Just listen…

"I will never leave you" (Hebrews 13:6).
"I will bear your burdens" (Psalm 68:19).
"I will forgive you" (1 John 1:9).
"I will make all things work together for good" (Romans 8:28).

And the promises go on and on.

Do What's Right

To walk uprightly, in the most basic sense, is to live a life that is characterized by doing what's right. It's recognizing the correct moral standard as the Word of God and living by it. Not that we live perfectly, but that we know our standard and we base our decisions, our actions, and our ambitions on what it teaches. Through the Word we are continually mindful of God's love for us, his will for us, and his promises for us, and our confidence in those things motivates us to try our very best to live uprightly.

The Scriptures, given by the Inspiration of God, provide us training in righteousness (2 Timothy 3:16). When we don't know what they teach we can be mistaken, or deceived, like the Sadducees (Mark 12:24). It is through God's Word that we come to know his commandments and his instructions (John 14:23-24), and because we love him, we obey him (John 14:15). God has given us everything we need to know that pertains to life and godliness through the knowledge of him, and our knowledge of him comes by way of his Word. If we read and study his Word, we can learn what is right and what is wrong; what is true and what is not.

Part of doing the right thing is knowing how to handle the temptations that we encounter every day. It makes me think about the years I spent in cardiac nursing working with patients in the early and advanced stages of cardiovascular disease. In caring for those patients, I developed a greater appreciation of the body's ability to self-heal and its built-in responses that compensate when other systems fail. I took special interest in the role of the sympathetic nervous system, and its effect which is commonly referred to as the "fight-or-flight" response.

When we find ourselves faced with difficult, dangerous, or stressful situations, the sympathetic nervous system is activated. Through a series of nerve impulses and the subsequent release of hormones, our bodies experience a variety of physical changes, including an increase in heart rate, an increase in blood pressure, an increase in sweat production, an increase in respiratory rate, and pupil dilation. These changes are designed to help us survive threatening situations by preparing us to either fight for our lives or run for our lives!

When I consider this amazing God-given capability within our human bodies, I can't help but recognize a spiritual application for the Christian. The Bible describes a type of "fight or flight" response when we, as children of God, are faced with the threat of temptation. Confronted with certain temptations, we must stand ready to fight, but there are other situations in which we are simply commanded to run.

The apostle Paul, when writing to the church at Corinth and later in letters to young Timothy, encouraged those Christians to run from temptation. He instructed them to flee:

- sexual immorality (1 Corinthians 6:18)
- idolatry (1 Corinthians 10:14)
- the love of money (1 Timothy 6:9-11)
- youthful lusts (2 Timothy 2:22)

There are times when our first response should be to immediately remove ourselves from the threat. Run away! Remember the story in the Bible of Joseph and Potiphar's wife:

"But it happened about this time, when Joseph went into the house to do his work, and none of the men of the house was inside, that she caught him by his garment, saying, 'Lie with me.' But he left his garment in her hand, and fled and ran outside" (Genesis 39:11-12).

But running is not always the appropriate response. At times, we face circumstances that require us to fight! We are exhorted in scripture to *"earnestly contend for the faith"* (Jude 1:3). In other words, fight for what you believe! We are also told, *"Therefore submit to God. Resist the devil and he will flee from you"* (James 4:7). Stand firm against the actions of the devil and *he* will run from *you*!

Fighting or fleeing; both take courage, both take preparation, and both are important actions when it comes to doing the right thing.

Learning to walk takes practice, instruction, and encouragement. Living uprightly works the same way: it takes practice, instruction, and encouragement. Sometimes we'll wobble, sometimes we might even fall, but we get up and we keep trying. As we continue to put one foot in front of the other, we continue moving forward.

Live by Faith

A little one is encouraged to take those first steps and what follows is a lifetime of walking. The same is true of upright living. It's a lifelong process. We don't just master it and then move on to something else! It is a constant aim; a continual effort. It's living by faith and reassuring your heart every day of the Truth. Our belief in God and his Word, along with our hope for a home in Heaven, should inspire us to live in a way that is upright; not just for one day, or one year, or one season of our life, but until the moment we reach our Promised Land.

Living by faith is demonstrating confidence in God and expecting him to do all that he has promised. It is your motivation to do what's right. It's the reason you obey, the reason you trust, the reason you keep on keeping on when you just want to stay on the floor and crawl.

Living by faith encourages you to daily ask yourself the questions, "What is it that I truly want? What am I looking for?" Is your answer "to go to Heaven"? If it is, then you must carefully consider how the choices you make will influence your eternity.

Living by faith means accepting the things that God has said, simply because he said them. It's living a life that is motivated by love for him and characterized by obedience to him. That's biblical faith! Even though you may not understand the things that happen in this life, you recognize that his ways are higher than your ways, his thoughts are higher than your thoughts…and you trust him (Isaiah 55:8-9).

Living by faith does not mean that upright living comes easy. Sometimes we might need a chair—something to lean on, something to get us from Point A to Point B without falling or without getting discouraged. Briggs' chair had a seat and four wooden legs, but our chairs might look more like the shoulder of a friend, or the prayers of our church family. To remain upright, we don't have to walk alone; we can rest our weight on other faithful travelers who are walking through the Wilderness toward the same destination. We hold each other up, help each other step, and keep each other strong.

A WALKING WARRIOR

"There was a man in the land of Uz, whose name was Job; and that man was blameless and upright, and one who feared God and shunned evil" (Job 1:1), and with those words, Job's story begins. The Book of Job is the first of the poetic books in the Old Testament and is widely referred to among religious and secular groups as a "masterpiece of literature." Victor Hugo is known to have said, "Tomorrow, if all literature was to be destroyed and it was left to me to retain one work only, I should save Job." It's true that the book itself is complex and beautifully written, but another part of its appeal is that the storyline resonates timelessly with mankind. Job's story is one of loss, suffering, faith, and mercy—all of which unfold under the cover of God's sovereign rule; and through it all, Job remains righteous!

Job endured a period of trial in his life that is difficult to comprehend. He suffered and suffered again. He faced financial ruin, illness, and death to a degree that seems unbearable. But what we find in Job is a man who walked uprightly before his trial, during his trial, and after his trial. How did he do it? He certainly didn't have help from his three friends: Eliphaz, Bildad, and Zophar!

At first Job's friends came and sat with him; and for seven days they didn't say a word, but cried with him in his anguish. In that expression of love and support, we learn a meaningful lesson from the friends about how to "mourn with those who mourn" (Romans 12:15); but when they open their mouths, it's a completely different story. Job's friends accused him of wrong-doing, believing that surely Job must have sinned to be judged so harshly by God. They urged him to repent so that he might receive God's blessings again.

Job called Eliphaz, Bildad, and Zophar "miserable comforters" (Job 16:2), and ultimately the men were condemned by God for not speaking what was right (Job 42:7-9). It's a good thing that Job had three other friends who helped him live through those dark days. These friends were with Job before his trial, during his trial, and after his trial. They were the reason he walked uprightly from verse one through the final words we read in Job 42:17, *"So Job died, old and full of days."* Those three dependable and virtuous friends of Job's were: *Patience, Trust, and Faith.*

Job's Three (Helpful) Friends

PATIENCE. This friend helped Job remain steadfast when everything he had was taken away. We tend to think of patience as the ability to wait for something that we want without getting upset or annoyed. This is not incorrect, but the Greek word, *hupomone*, that is often translated "patience" in our English Bibles, carries a richer meaning. The preposition *hupo* means "under," and *meno* means "to remain or to abide," so *hupomeno* represents the idea of "remaining under" something. When it's used in reference to difficulties or trials, the illustration is of one who is able to stand strong, without wavering, under the pressures of life and will even use those experiences to bring glory to God.

Job's friend, Patience, kept him from giving up and crumpling under the weight of his trials. It enabled him to overcome. Patience was not a weak friend; it provided Job with the strength and fortitude to persevere.

In his epistle, James, the brother of Jesus, wrote, *"My brethren, count it all joy when you fall into various trials, knowing that the testing of your faith produces patience. But let patience have its perfect work, that you may be perfect and complete, lacking in nothing"* (James 1:2-4).

Patience is our friend when our faith is tested. If we let it accomplish its purpose, patience will completely equip us with all that we need to reach our ultimate goal. Let patience walk with you to the Promised Land.

TRUST. This friend helped Job endure his trial even knowing that God's plan could result in his death. In Job 13:15 we read the words of Job, *"Though He slay me, yet will I trust Him."* The Hebrew word for "trust" in this context is *yachal*, and can also be translated "wait, hope, or expect." If death were to come, Job's hope would continue to rest in God.

It was Trust who placed these words in the heart of Job, *"Look, I go forward, but He is not there, and backward, but I cannot perceive Him; when He works on the left hand, I cannot behold Him; when He turns to the right hand, I cannot see Him. But He knows the way that I take; when He has tested me, I shall come forth as gold"* (Job 23:8-10).

Job's friend, Trust, reminded him that God was in control. When God rebuked Job for questioning him, it was because of trust that Job repented with this prayer to God, *"I know that You can do everything, and that no purpose of Yours can be withheld from You. You asked, 'Who is this who hides counsel without knowledge?' Therefore I have uttered what I did not understand. Things too wonderful for me, which I did not know. Listen, please, and let me speak; You said, 'I will question you, and you shall answer me.' I have heard of You by the hearing of the ear, but now my eye sees You. Therefore, I abhor myself and repent in dust and ashes"* (Job 42:2-6).

Trust is our friend, too. It will teach us not to depend on our understanding, and if we keep it in our hearts, God will direct our paths (Proverbs 3:5-6). Trust is a necessary travel companion to have with us on this journey!

FAITH. This friend helped Job understand that God is in control—in the good times and in the times of trouble. Faith stood by Job as he offered sacrifices on behalf of his sons and daughters; Faith also held Job up as he cried over the graves of those same children. Faith stood by Job as he was recognized as the "greatest of all the people of the East" (Job 1:3); Faith also held Job up as he scraped the painful sores that covered his body from head to foot. When Job's wife told him to *"Curse God and die!"* it was because of Faith that Job could say, *"You speak as one of the foolish women speaks. Shall we indeed accept good from God, and shall we not accept adversity?"* (Job 2:9-10).

Faith was there when Eliphaz, Bildad, and Zophar accused Job of sin and called on him to repent. Faith was there when Job was at the end of his line and there was nowhere else to turn but to the eternal grave or to the eternal God. It was because of his friend, Faith, that Job was able to proclaim in the middle of his torment: *"For I know that my Redeemer lives, and He shall stand at last on the earth"* (Job 19:25). Faith kept Job's eyes focused on God.

Make faith your friend in every chapter of life. It is a valuable friendship—one with eternal reward. Peter said, *"In this you greatly rejoice, though now for a little while, if need be, you have been grieved by various trials, that the genuineness of your faith, being much more precious than gold that perishes, though it is tested by fire, may be found to praise, honor, and glory at the revelation of Jesus Christ, whom having not seen you love. Though now you do not see Him, yet believing, you rejoice with joy inexpressible and full of glory, receiving the end of your faith—the salvation of your souls"* (1 Peter 1:6-9).

Job's three friends, Patience, Trust, and Faith, helped him through his darkest days. He endured and was ultimately rewarded because of their role in his life. It's important to understand that his relationship with them had been established and nurtured long before his trials came. His friends served him well when he needed them the most because he wasn't a stranger to them. They had been helping him walk uprightly throughout his life, even in the good times. Patience, Trust, and Faith knew Job! He had *always* been their friend.

IN HIS STEPS

Jesus lived a perfect life for thirty-three years on this earth. He was subjected to temptations, but never yielded. I imagine that Satan tried very hard to make our Savior commit sin. After all, if Satan could make Jesus stumble—with just one sinful thought or just one careless word—the plan for our redemption would be ruined. The perfect Lamb would no longer be perfect, and the blood would lose its power to remove sin. We should express our gratitude every day for the righteousness of Jesus. His perfect life fulfilled the perfect plan to give us perfect hope for a perfect place. Praise God!

"For we do not have a High Priest who cannot _____ with our weaknesses, but was in all points _____ as we are, yet without _____" (Hebrews 4:15).

OUR DAILY WALK _____

Living uprightly begins in the heart. It's the desire to be in the presence of God. It's a yearning to look on his face and for him to look on yours. It's wanting to fall into his arms at the end of our wilderness journey. It's taking every step in the direction that brings us closer and closer to his embrace.

Living uprightly involves doing what's right. It's following the Word of God. It's standing on his Truth. It's knowing when to fight and when to run. It's understanding that we will wobble, we might even fall, but we get back up, and we keep on trying.

Living uprightly is living by faith. It's continually placing our confidence in God and in his Word. It's allowing him to lead us and trusting him when it seems we are sinking in the sands of the wilderness. It's how we live when living is hard.

To walk uprightly we have to begin each day with a renewed effort to "bring every thought into captivity to the obedience of Christ" (2 Corinthians 10:5). Control your mind. Before you step out of bed, decide that your day is going to be lived to God's glory. Resolve to nurture your friendship with patience, trust, and faith. Uphold them on the good days so they can uphold you when the hard days come.

What can we do to live uprightly from day to day?

We can pray. *"Watch and pray, lest you enter into temptation. The spirit indeed is willing, but the flesh is weak"* (Mark 14:38).

We can read and study the Word of God. *"Blessed are the undefiled in the way, who walk in the law of the Lord! Blessed are those who keep His testimonies, who seek Him with the whole heart! They also do no iniquity; they walk in His ways"* (Psalm 119:1-3).

We can recognize our weaknesses. *"But each one is tempted when he is drawn away by his own desires and enticed"* (James 1:14). When we know the areas where we struggle to remain upright, we can prepare for them and develop a battle plan for fighting off those temptations.

We can confess our sins to one another. *"Confess your trespasses to one another, and pray for one another, that you may be healed"* (James 5:16). Lean on your brothers and sisters in Christ in order to walk tall. Let them be your chair—and you be a chair for others. Pray for each other!

STRENGTH

How can you develop a heart that yearns for Christ?

The time to start practicing patience, trust, and faith is right now. Don't wait until you are standing in ashes and covered in sores with nothing left before you call on them for help! A person who is living uprightly will be patient, trusting, and faithful before the trials come as well as when the trials are barging through the door.

How do you demonstrate your faith on a normal-everyday-kind of day?

How about your patience?

Your trust?

TRIALS

What, or who, are your chairs?

In this chapter, we talked about how there are some temptations you can fight, but in some cases when you are faced with a temptation, you need to run. What temptations do you find yourself fighting on your daily walk? Which ones make you run?

Job's three friends—Patience, Trust, and Faith—helped him endure his trials. What other virtuous friends help us remain upright during trials?

ENCOURAGEMENT

Think of someone you know who is going through a difficult time. It might be someone who is fighting a disease or someone who has recently lost a loved one. It might be someone who is struggling through school, or trying to find a job. It might be someone whose marriage has ended or who is battling depression.

Take some time to send a note of encouragement to that person. Job desperately needed kind and thoughtful friends.

Think of someone who might be lonely. Think of someone who might be in mourning.

Take some time to go and sit with that person. Remember the quiet comfort Job's three friends provided when they first arrived at his side.

Think of someone who is suffering, hurting, or questioning their faith.

Take some time to pray for that person. What a loving support the prayers of friends would have been to Job's troubled spirit. *"The effective, fervent prayer of a righteous man avails much"* (James 5:16).

PRAYER

Sovereign God and Creator of all things, I humbly come before your throne in my weakness and imperfection. I am thankful for the honor of being in your presence through prayer, and I beg your forgiveness for my sins.

Although I am weak, I know that you will make me strong. Although I am imperfect, I know that you are continuing a good work in me that won't be completed until Jesus comes again.

Help me to patiently wait for you. Help me to trust in your will for my life. Help me to faithfully endure times of trial. I hope that I can be like Job and live upright and blameless before you.

Fill me with your strength so that I can stand straight and walk tall.

In Jesus' Name, Amen

WALK WITH THE DOC

Walking tip: Walk uprightly

Take a moment, look around, and you will see that a large percentage of our day is spent with our head down: working at a desk, using a cell phone, laptop or tablet, etc. Even while watching television or resting on a pillow in bed, our necks are somewhat flexed. Our posture suffers as a result and puts us at risk of developing spinal issues, such as osteoarthritis, later in life. Walking uprightly can reduce that risk. When walking, follow these basic steps: stand up straight, do not lean forward or back, keep your eyes looking forward at a distance of 10-20 feet, keep your chin up, shrug your shoulders and let them fall naturally. Not only will your posture improve, but you will breathe easier and have less back pain. Walk often and walk tall.

TAKE ACTION!

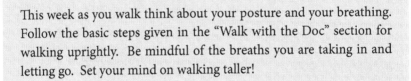

This week as you walk think about your posture and your breathing. Follow the basic steps given in the "Walk with the Doc" section for walking uprightly. Be mindful of the breaths you are taking in and letting go. Set your mind on walking taller!

CHAPTER TEN

CHOOSE WISELY

Walk with Wise Men

"He who walks with wise men will be wise, but the companion of fools will be destroyed" (Proverbs 13:20).

There's a story I heard recently that I will never forget. My family and I were at the Crieve Hall church of Christ in Nashville, Tennessee celebrating the 50th Anniversary of the Nashville School of Preaching and enjoying presentations by a variety of men with close connections to the school. One speaker shared an account about Hugo McCord, a Christian man who is remembered as a writer, teacher, and Gospel preacher.

He had been holding a meeting near Jasper, Alabama. As customary, he was invited into the homes of Christians in the area and provided with food and a place to sleep. One evening, he found himself sitting at a table in the home of a woman who had a young son. It was clear that the woman did not have much money, and when it came time to serve supper, she humbly placed a bowl of beans in front of Brother McCord. She apologized for the simple meal and said this to her honored guest: *"I just wanted my son to sit close to you."*

She didn't have much to give, but she gave what she had for the opportunity to bring a faithful servant of God into her home and into the life of her son. She wanted her son to be near Brother McCord; she wanted her son to be influenced by his words and his character. That woman understood the importance of wise men and the value of their influence.

I know Christian men and women like that, and I'm sure you do, too. You find that you are blessed just being around them! People who make you want to be better, become stronger, and do more. These are people who so love the Word of God that they immerse themselves in it, and they live it! Then they reach out to help others by sharing it and teaching it! You can't help but see the Spirit of God working through their lives in the passionate way they study and apply the Scriptures to their daily walk. Oh, to be someone whose very presence encourages others to be better walkers!

Friend-fluence

"Friend-fluence" – *noun*, the ability of our friends to have an effect on our character, development, or behavior.

Our friends can build us up, or they can tear us down. They can point the way to Jesus, or they can lead us in the wrong direction. Friends have the power to shape the very quality of who we are as Christians. The Bible warns us to choose them carefully (Proverbs 12:26). Evil friends will corrupt good morals, but wise friends will help us become wise as well (1 Corinthians 15:33, Proverbs 13:20).

There is a saying that appears frequently in different forms but the idea is always the same, "Show me his company, and I'll tell you the man." Simply put, we become the people that we hang around. God knew this to be true and ordered for the people of Canaan to be completely driven out of the land before the Israelites settled there. In Numbers 33:55, he said this to Moses, *"But if you do not drive out the inhabitants of the land from before you, then it shall be that those whom you let remain shall be irritants in your eyes and thorns in your sides, and they shall harass you in the land where you dwell."*

God knew what would happen to his people under the influence of the Canaanites. They would become unfaithful, they would turn to idols, and they would adopt some of the same disgraceful practices in the name of a false religion. God knew it would happen, and it did.

The importance of faithful and wise friends cannot be underestimated. You have to be proactive when it comes to friendships. Choose friends who will strengthen you and help you grow spiritually. Don't continue in a friendship that will lead to wilderness wandering! Help people? Yes! Be kind to people? Always! Nurture friendships that lead you away from the Lord? Never!

Imagine for a moment that you are a car. Right now, you're not walking through the wilderness; you are *racing*! The desert sands have been replaced by asphalt, and as you drive, you're looking for travel buddies. Before you swing open your doors to just anyone, consider the qualities of your company.

Pit Crew or Chop Shop

In a race, your pit crew is made up of the people who service or refuel your car. They might check your tires or your engine, and if anything needs repairing, they will fix you right up. After a quick stop, you are ready to rejoin the race and are better than you were before you checked in with your pit crew.

A chop shop, on the other hand, doesn't have such kind ambitions. They take apart stolen cars for the purpose of selling their parts. They look at each car for its potential worth and are only interested in personal gain.

Are your friends a part of your pit crew, or are they the owners of a chop shop?

Like a pit crew, your friends should build you up, keep you going, and repair you when you're broken. A good friend will get you back on track if you lose control. They refuel you and might even give you a shine. They are concerned for your safety, so they check your engine and the tread on your tires.

Listen to what the Bible says about friends:

"Two are better than one, because they have a good reward for their labor. For if they fall, one will lift up his companion, but woe to him who is alone when he falls, for he has no one to help him up" (Ecclesiastes 4:9-10).

"A friend loves at all times, and a brother is born for adversity" (Proverbs 17:17).

"As iron sharpens iron, so a man sharpens the countenance of his friend" (Proverbs 27:17).

The righteous should choose his friends carefully, for the way of the wicked leads them astray" (Proverbs 12:26).

Do your friends sincerely care about you? Do they care about your *soul*? If they do, then they will edify you with the Word, they will encourage you when your faith is weak, and they will help you when you're struggling with sin. They will fill you up with gracious words, they will forgive you when you mess up, and they will love you on the days when you are less than lovable. After spending time with them, you leave feeling happier and stronger than you were before.

Chop shop friends will tear you down. Pit crew friends will do everything they can to make you a better traveler. Do you have a pit crew? If not, it's never too late to start gathering a team!

Road Signs or Backseat Drivers

Road signs point the way. They are dependable. Their purpose is to help you get where you are going. Backseat drivers? Not so much. They interfere without knowledge and tend to offer unwanted advice. *And* they criticize.

Do your friends serve as road signs, or are they backseat drivers?

Like road signs, our friends provide us with direction. Good friends will point you to Jesus; their guidance will lead you closer to the finish line. When you're lost, you can rely on them to show you the right way. They advise you when to stop, when to slow down, when to take a detour, and when danger is expected on the road up ahead. They are there for you, rain or shine! They are always helpful and always truthful. Here is what the Bible tells us about road sign friends:

"Ointment and perfume delight the heart, and the sweetness of a man's friend gives delight by hearty counsel" (Proverbs 27:9).

"Blessed is the man who walks not in the counsel of the ungodly, nor stands in the path of sinners, nor sits in the seat of the scornful" (Psalm 1:1).

The Bible has quite different words to say about friends who act more like backseat drivers:

"Go from the presence of a foolish man, when you do not perceive in him the lips of knowledge" (Proverbs 14:7).

"A fool has no delight in understanding, but in expressing his own heart"

(Proverbs 18:2).

"Even when a fool walks along the way, he lacks wisdom, and he shows everyone that he is a fool" (Ecclesiastes 10:3).

Backseat driver friends think more about themselves than the person who is driving. They put great emphasis on their own personal ideas and opinions, and they aren't too worried about the facts or where you'll end up in the long run. They can be outright dangerous.

Road sign friends want to help you get to Heaven! They don't want to see you wandering around in the wilderness or traveling in the opposite direction of the Promised Land. They are faithful guides and have your best interests at heart. Do you have these types of friends in your life? We all need them lining our roadsides!

A WALKING WARRIOR

In the book of Mark there is a two verse account of a situation that takes place immediately after the arrest of Jesus in the Garden of Gethsemane.

"Now a certain young man followed Him, having a linen cloth thrown around his naked body. And the young men laid hold of him, and he left the linen cloth and fled from them naked" (Mark 14:51-52).

Many Bible scholars agree that this "certain young man" was actually Mark, himself! The main reason for coming to this conclusion is that no other Gospel mentions this story. Mark is the only one who includes the brief account of the mystery runner. Also, Mark's mother lived in Jerusalem, and it's possible that he was staying at her home when he heard of Jesus' impending arrest; then ran from the house, grabbing just a linen cloth on his way out the door. It's only speculation, but interesting to think about. The tragic point is that Jesus was deserted by all of his followers when he needed them the most.

Whether the "certain young man" was Mark or not, there is another story in which Mark undoubtedly runs away from a difficult situation; but in the end, because of the friends and mentors he chose to walk with, Mark grew from a frightened follower into a faithful fighter!

Mark and Peter

We are first introduced to Mark in the 13th chapter of Acts. He is identified in verse 12 as "John whose surname was Mark," and from that point on he is referred to in Scripture simply as "Mark." We are also told in verse 12 that he was the son of a woman named Mary, and many people were gathered at her home in Jerusalem for the purpose of praying together. We can know just from this glimpse at Mark that he was influenced by a Christian mother and a faithful home.

Mark 13:12 falls right in the middle of an amazing story about the apostle Peter, and to understand more about Mark, we need to take a look at what was happening on this occasion that had brought people together to pray in the home of his mother.

In 45 A.D., under the direction of King Herod Agrippa the church continued to suffer persecution. He had James, the brother of John, executed and when he saw that it pleased the Jews, he had Peter arrested as well. Herod's plan was to have Peter murdered in front of the people after Passover, but God had a much different plan.

The night before Peter was scheduled to be brought in front of the Jewish people to meet the same fate as his friend and fellow disciple, James, an angel appeared in the prison and miraculously helped him escape. When Peter realized what had happened *("An angel of The Lord just saved my life!")* he went to the house of Mary, where members of the church were meeting together to pray over his safety.

From this story, we know that Mark had an association with Peter. We know that Peter chose the house of Mark's mother to go for safety when his life was in danger, and it's likely that he had been there before. Later, the relationship between Mark and Peter would grow closer and prove very meaningful in the development of Mark's character and his faith.

Mark and Barnabas

Barnabas, the man we know as "The Son of Encouragement" (Acts 4:36), had a special connection to John Mark. The two men were cousins, and it becomes clear through Scripture that the influence Barnabas had on the life of Mark was invaluable. In Acts 12:25 through 13:13, we read how these men joined Paul on his first missionary journey, but the outcome for Mark was not a favorable one—in fact, his leg of the trip ended in a way that would haunt him later.

Paul and Barnabas had just traveled back to Antioch after delivering relief to the Christians in Jerusalem, but they hadn't returned alone. They had brought John Mark along with them. At some point during their stay in Jerusalem, Paul and Barnabas had encountered Mark and something about his character landed him a seat on the boat headed to Antioch. It may have been that Barnabas suggested he join them; Mark was part of his family, and he may have believed in Mark's ability to provide them with help on the trip, but the Bible does not say specifically how he was chosen.

Once in Antioch, Paul and Barnabas ministered along with other prophets and teachers until the Holy Spirit set them apart for a special work. They were to leave Antioch and carry the Gospel to other areas in the region. The first stop of the first missionary journey was on the island of Cyprus. Acts 13:5 tells us that Mark was still with them, serving as their assistant.

After preaching the word of God in Salamis, they traveled to the other side of the island, to a city called Paphos. In Paphos they ran into some trouble. A sorcerer, named Elymas, opposed their teaching and tried to prevent the spreading of the Gospel. He was strongly rebuked by Paul and struck with blindness for a period of time. It is also believed that Paul may have contracted some kind of illness while on the island because he makes reference in his Galatian letter to a "physical infirmity" (Galatians 4:13), and the area of Galatia is where he traveled after visiting Cyprus.

All of this, including the threat of persecution and the difficulties that would surely arise related to transportation, food, and shelter, proved too much for Mark. He wanted out. When the team arrived in Perga, Mark returned to Jerusalem. He was fearful and went back home. Paul and Barnabas continued their trip, and the church grew.

A few years later in the city of Antioch, Paul suggested to Barnabas that they begin another journey, this time with the purpose of going back and visiting all of the cities where the Word had been preached. Mark's name came up again. Barnabas was determined to take him on the trip, but Paul passionately disagreed. He reminded Barnabas that Mark had deserted them and that he had not gone with them to do the work he had set out to do. The contention between Paul and Barnabas was sharp, and they decided to part ways. Paul chose Silas to join him and Barnabas took Mark.

Mark was blessed to have a wise and compassionate friend like Barnabas, a friend who recognized extraordinary potential and who believed in second chances. Under the wing of Barnabas, Mark would be trained, strengthened, and encouraged. In Acts 15:39, we read that Barnabas and Mark sailed to Cyprus and ten years passed before Mark's name was mentioned again.

Mark and Paul

In the years 60-62 A.D., Paul was under house arrest in Rome. We can read about the events that resulted in his arrest in the latter part of Acts 21. While in Rome, Paul wrote the books of Ephesians, Philippians, Colossians, and Philemon, collectively known as the prison epistles. In his letter to the church in Colossae, Paul referred to Mark as his "fellow worker" and said that he had "proved to be a comfort" to him (Colossians 4:10-11). In Philemon 24, he again called Mark his "fellow worker."

Paul's final imprisonment occurred between the years 64 and 66 A.D. During that time, Paul wrote two letters to Timothy and one letter to Titus. In his second letter to Timothy, and the final correspondence made by Paul before he was martyred, he sent for Mark. In 2 Timothy 4:11, Paul wrote, *"Only Luke is with me. Get Mark and bring him with you, for he is useful to me for ministry."*

It's evident from the letters written by Paul during his time in Rome that his attitude toward Mark was different. What had changed? How did Mark turn from a deserter into a fellow laborer and become useful to the greatest missionary to ever live?

It has everything to do with the friends Mark chose!

We already know that he was mentored by the faithful and kind Barnabas. We also find in Scripture that at some point after his desertion, Mark developed a closer relationship with the great apostle Peter (1 Peter 5:13). He was with Peter in Rome at the time 1 and 2 Peter were written; and in the first letter, Peter sent greetings to the readers on behalf of Mark, whom he referred to as "my son." While there in Rome, Mark had contact with Paul and was able to mend their relationship as well as demonstrate to Paul that he had the heart and spirit of a disciple of Christ.

Many scholars believe that the time Mark spent with Peter strongly influenced the writing and content of the Gospel of Mark. When we first meet Mark in Acts 12 and 13, we might describe him as fearful, untrusting, and some might even say a coward. He deserted his mission team and went home, but he didn't remain there for long. He made some decisions about the person he wanted to become, and he chose some people who could help him get there. And he didn't choose small—he chose the biggest names of the time: Barnabas, Peter, and Paul!

The wise friends Mark associated with helped him become useful in ministry. He grew under the direction of three giants of faith. Peter certainly knew how it felt to be a deserter! He understood the shame that came with that title, and he built Mark up. He trained him, worked with him, guided him, and grew him into another giant of faith. Many scholars believe that

IN HIS STEPS

"You are My friends if you do whatever I command you. No longer do I call you servants, for a servant does not know what his master is doing; but I have called you _____ _____, for all things that I heard from My Father I have made known to you. You did not choose Me, but ____ _____ _____ and appointed you that you should go and bear fruit, and that your fruit should remain, that whatever you _____ the Father in My name He may _____ you. These things I command you, that you _____ one another" (John 15:12-16).

Jesus chose his friends carefully and prayerfully. Before he named his apostles, Jesus spent the entire night in prayer to God. The men he selected were not perfect, but with the exception of Judas, they all faithfully carried out his mission to seek and save the lost after he returned to Heaven. They suffered in his name and were martyred in his name. Jesus' friends were obedient, loving, and devoted to him. He chose them well; even Judas was used providentially to accomplish God's plan. What a privilege to be considered a friend of Jesus!

the time Mark spent with Peter had a great impact on the writing and content of the Gospel of Mark.

Never, never underestimate the power of godly influences!

OUR DAILY WALK

When Desert Shield evolved into Desert Storm, the winds of war had carried my dad to the Middle East. As the Command Surgeon of the Air Force at Central Command, he traveled with General Schwarzkopf to Saudi Arabia and was stationed with him in the capital city of Riyadh for the duration of the conflict. It was a frightening time for our family.

My dad, who the General referred to as "Doc," was in charge of the medical support that was provided to the brave men and women who risked their lives for the cause of freedom and justice. Although he wasn't on the front lines of battle, he certainly lived under the threat of airstrikes, and he called us regularly, which was a blessing, and would keep us updated on any developments that he was able to share.

It had been a long year, but the conflict had ended and Dad was coming home! There was a big welcome home ceremony prepared and all of the families of the members of Central Command were invited out to the flight line to welcome home their family members. My mom, my sisters, and I were beyond excited! When we finally saw Dad step off the plane we swarmed him and there was a lot of hugging, crying, laughing, and more hugging. We were incredibly thankful to have him home.

A platform and podium had been set up for General Schwarzkopf to make a statement after his arrival and the media were there in droves. After he greeted his family and spent a few minutes talking with them, he was directed toward the platform. His family was ushered up there alongside him and the cameras were going crazy.

Somewhere, somehow, in all of the hustle and bustle, my younger sister Julia got mixed in with the Schwarzkopf family. She was hurried up onto the platform with the rest of them, and the next thing we know, our family is looking up at the Schwarzkopf family, and there's Julia, standing right in the middle of them! The next day, the front page of the newspaper had a big

picture of the General giving his remarks at the flight line with his family...
and Julia...right by his side.

Years later, at a Freed-Hardeman benefit dinner, Julia saw General Schwarzkopf again, and when he saw her, he exclaimed, "Well, there's my long lost
daughter!"

I told you that story for this daily walking reminder: Be careful who you
position yourself next to as you travel to the Promised Land. It doesn't take
much to get carried into a situation that is spinning out of control simply
because of who you choose to walk with along with way. One minute you
might be standing close beside someone, and then the next minute you're
on the front page of the paper as a member of their family! Or, like Lot, one
minute you're pitching your tent near an evil city, and the next minute you're
being visited at your home there by two angels with a terrifying message of
destruction (Genesis 19).

Be careful when choosing your friends. Choose wisely.

STRENGTH

Proverbs 27:17 says, *"As iron sharpens iron, so a man sharpens the
countenance of his friend."* **What does this mean, and how do we do
it?**

**How can friends help or hinder your travel on the wilderness jour-
ney?**

What do you think is the most important quality to have in a friend?

What makes a wise friend a good friend?

TRIALS

Some friends may seem wise according to the world's standards, but they don't have the "wisdom that is from above" (James 3:17). How can you tell the difference?

Take a look inside. What kind of a friend are you? Are you a wise friend? What can you do to become a pit crew member or a road sign for someone else?

How can we help the world come to know Jesus without being friends with the world?

ENCOURAGEMENT

Proverbs has been referred to as the "Book of Wisdom." Written mainly by Solomon, it's a book about how to live an effective life on this earth and contains short and practical instructions for finding wisdom. The theme of the book is found in the seventh verse of the first chapter: *"The fear of the Lord is the beginning of knowledge, but fools despise wisdom and instruction."*

Read the third chapter of Proverbs. From verse 13 through verse 26, the author specifically wrote about the virtue of wisdom. He mentioned a number of benefits that are received by those who are wise. Begin in verse 13, and make a list of the good things that come about as a result of finding wisdom and gaining understanding. (I've written down the first one!)

Blessings of wisdom:
1. Happiness

PRAYER

Gracious God, you are always faithful. You cover me with blessings every day. Thank you for taking care of me. I see evidence of your infinite goodness everywhere I look.

I ask that you give me wisdom. I need wisdom while I'm walking through this wilderness; wisdom for choosing travel companions; wisdom to stay on the path. I know that you will give it to me, if I believe; and I believe with all of my heart that you are able. With wisdom, I pray for humility as well. Help me to never forget who I am and where I would be without you.

Dear God, fill my life with good and wise friends. Bless me with friends who will point me to Jesus. Help me to empty my life of the people who pull me away from my eternal purpose.

Thank you for the gift of friendship.

In Jesus' Name, Amen

WALK WITH THE DOC

Walking tip: Walk to remember

Some fear dementia more than death. While death is certain, dementia, including memory loss, need not be in every instance. There are measures which can be taken to either prevent or mitigate the disease. The Latin phrase *mens sana in corpore sano* means "a sound mind in a sound body." A primary focus should be taking care of the body, which provides oxygen and nutrients to the brain. Vascular dementia is a result of the same disease process that causes decreased blood flow in the heart. The same measures to reduce heart disease apply to the brain. Hence, what's good for the heart is good for the brain. Walking promotes circulation, and reduces risk of coronary heart disease and vascular dementia. Fear of dementia can be substantially reduced by understanding the disease and pursuing measures, such as walking, that can prevent or delay the onset of age-related cognitive impairment or dementia.

TAKE ACTION!

Our minds are rarely quiet. Throughout the day we're constantly thinking, planning, organizing, creating, teaching, learning, and sometimes we just need to allow our brains some time to slow down. Walking provides a wonderful opportunity to clear your mind and meditate deeply on what is truly important.

Take a peaceful walk of reflection. Notice little things around you as you walk, and if you've been keeping a journal, write about your experience. Talk to God in prayer. Take in the beauty of nature. Do this often.

CHAPTER ELEVEN
LOVE. THAT'S ALL.
Walk in Love

"Therefore be imitators of God as dear children. And walk in love, as Christ also has loved us and given Himself for us, an offering and a sacrifice to God for a sweet-swelling aroma" (Ephesians 5:1-2).

"*D*o you know what it is?" Evie looked at me with an expression of unadulterated joy, her eyes open wide anticipating my answer. She had been going through a gift giving phase ever since her fourth birthday. She would take one of her baby blankets, wrap something inside it, and then give it to me, Sam, or Kate. As she was gift wrapping, she would say "cut, cut, cut; tape, tape, tape" expertly handling unseen scissors and rolls of scotch tape. Then, she would proudly hand it to one of us and say "I have a present for you!" Sometimes the gift was one of her favorite stuffed animals and sometimes it was a piece of her princess jewelry; you just never knew until you unfolded the blanket-paper.

This time when I opened the blanket, though, there was nothing inside. I must have looked a little confused, and Evie asked, "Do you know what it is?"

"No," I answered, "I don't see anything, Sweetie!"

"That's because it's *love!*" And with that, she threw her arms around me, gave me a kiss, and then ran off; leaving me with an empty blanket and the most precious gift I've ever been given.

Love. It's the basis of Christianity: Seeking the greatest good for another. Love can be defined in so many ways. If you asked a group of ten people for a definition of love, you might end up with ten different answers. When I think of love, I think of the One who gave his life for me. I think about Jesus and his life on earth. I think about how he helped people, how he showed compassion, and how he never quit the plan. He is our perfect example of love.

Cooperation

One night at the hospital I received a call from a nurse who needed help starting an IV on one of her patients. After walking into the patient's room and introducing myself, I realized that the patient was blind. He was resting in the hospital bed, and his wife stood intently by his side. I touched the patient's arm as I came closer to the bed and explained why I had been called to his room.

I began assembling my supplies, and I noticed that as I worked, the patient's wife talked to both me and her husband explaining to me their experience with IVs in the past and then also explaining to him everything that I was doing. She never left his side and continually enriched his awareness of what was happening all around him. The love and concern she had for her husband was inspiring. Undoubtedly, they had spent many years together and had perfected the art of partnership. She served as his eyes in a way that was not intrusive or degrading, but rather tender and supportive. As I secured the IV to his arm, he thanked me for coming, and she gushed about how relieved she felt to have that completed. It was as if it was just as difficult for her to be stuck as it was for him—and I believe it was!

I appreciated the reminder that this couple, unknowingly, gave: love amends and rectifies! Where one is weak, the other is strong. Where one is lacking, the other provides. Our physical bodies operate on this very concept. For example, when the body experiences significant blood loss, the cardiovascular system immediately puts into action processes that ensure adequate blood flow to our vital organs. Our bodies determine a need and do what is necessary to keep us alive.

In marriage as "two become one flesh" (1 Corinthians 6:16), this is how we should function, as well. When one partner suffers, physically, emotionally, or spiritually, the other steps in to render support, encouragement, and nurturing. Together, we do what is necessary to keep our marriage alive. It's a wonderful thing.

I left that hospital room deeply touched. Through this patient's blindness and his wife's vivid descriptions of the world around him, they created beautiful vision…together!

Cooperation, working with each other and helping each other, is a way to show our love for each other.

Compassion

My husband and I had been called in for a meeting at the school. Evie's teacher wanted to discuss her placement in the gifted program for middle school after reviewing the results from the most recent round of testing. The meeting would also include the principal, the counselor, and a Special Education teacher.

As we made our way into the conference room and began situating ourselves around a table, the Special Ed teacher looked at me and Sam and said, "Before we get started, I have to tell you a story about Evie—something I saw on the playground the other day."

For the last few weeks, Evie had been telling me all about recess. A big group of kids in her grade had started playing baseball during their time outside, and Evie was loving it! She would get in the car at the end of the school day and right away begin filling me in on who played what position, who hit the homerun, who got mad, and who won. She would get so excited just talking about it! Evie looked forward to recess ball every day.

The teacher began telling us her story…

"Last week, while the students were playing baseball on the playground, one of our Special Education students walked over to the team that was up to bat and asked if he could play. All of the kids started yelling 'No! You can't play on our team! Go ask the other team!' So he *did* ask the other team, and the kids in the outfield started yelling the same things, 'No! You can't play with us! Go ask the other team!'"

"It was heartbreaking. After a couple rounds of back and forth rejection, he turned to walk away, with his little shoulders slumped over, and that's when I saw Evie. She had stepped out of the batting line and caught up with the student. She put her arm around him and said, 'Come on! You can be on MY team!' She turned him back toward the field, guided him back to her spot in line, and stood him right next to her, just daring anyone to say anything. Nobody said a word."

"I wanted to tell you that I was proud of her. It made me so happy to see her stand up for someone who was being mistreated. She has such a good heart."

I was speechless! The first reason is because I was overwhelmed with love and appreciation for my sweet daughter. The second reason is because I can't understand how people can be so mean. And finally, I was speechless because Evie never told me that story.

She never mentioned it when she gushed with details over how many runs each team scored, or who struck out, or who was pitching. She never told me about how she saved someone's day…or week…or year. She just did it.

She just did it, because that's Evie. It's her nature. She walks in compassion.

To show someone compassion is to show them love.

Commitment

I don't remember what brought me into her hospital room that night but what I do recall is the look of fear on her face as I approached her bed. Her back, shoulders, and neck were rigid, keeping her from relaxing back against the pillow, and her hands grasped the top edge of the sheets that she had drawn up to her chin. She looked like a scared child, but the whistle blowing silver of her hair and tattling lines on her face revealed an age of near ninety.

Trying to help calm her, I introduced myself and reassured her that we would be taking good care of her while in the hospital. Since she kept glancing toward the door, I asked if she had family that had come with her to the Emergency Room. At that, I heard a voice come from the far corner. It startled me as I hadn't seen anyone else in the room when I first entered.

"I'm here," someone said. I turned and saw an elderly man slowly rise from the couch in the darkness. Hearing his words, the patient sat up straighter and nervously responded, "Who is that?" Wondering the same thing, I asked the man how he was related to the patient. "I'm her husband. We've been married 60 years. She knows I'm here." Then (loud enough for the patient to hear) he said, "I'm always here." The patient eased back into her pillow, her hands loosened their hold on the sheet, and she closed her eyes as relief flooded her body. I say "flooded" because it spilled over to me as I simply stood next to her.

As this woman found comfort in the presence of her life partner, so we can find comfort in the presence of our Life Giver. He, himself, has said, "I will never leave you nor forsake you" (Hebrews 13:5). Taking a deeper look at this Scripture, I found that the Greek word used here for "forsake" is *egkataleipo.* This word carries the meaning "to abandon, to desert, to leave helpless, to leave in straits, to leave in a lurch, or let one down." In the Greek text, it is also preceded by three negatives which essentially multiplies the power of the promise, "I will not, I will not, I will not abandon you, desert you, leave you helpless or let you down." Those are the words of our God, our Heavenly Father, our Savior. He is *always* with us.

I forget this promise sometimes. Occasionally, my son jogs my memory as we drive down the road and he asks, "Mom, is God in the car with us right now?" On one particular night, it was a fearful patient and her loving husband who reminded me that I am never alone and the true peace that can be found in knowing that (*Trailblazers*, p. 105-106).

Love never leaves. Love is commitment.

A WALKING WARRIOR

On May 9th, 1998, I stood next to the man I fell heart-and-soul in love with, in front of a large group of our family and friends, and said these words: *"Entreat me not to leave you, or to turn back from following after you; for wherever you go, I will go; and wherever you lodge, I will lodge; your people shall be my people, and your God, my God. Where you die, I will die, and there I will be buried. The Lord do so to me, and more also, if anything but death parts you and me"* (Ruth 1:16-17). I meant every word then, and I mean every word today. I still love that man with all of my heart and soul!

Faithful devotion continues to ring true in those words that were spoken thousands of years ago by a woman named Ruth as she vowed to stay with her mother-in-law, Naomi, following the death of her husband. The love between those two women led to another love story, which parallels a divine love story—with an ending that continues to affect lives happily eternally after.

Ruth and Naomi

Naomi grieved for her husband and sons. A widow, in a foreign land, with two widowed daughters-in-law, what hope did she have for the future? All she could do was to return empty-handed to her homeland and fall on the mercy of her people. She urged Ruth and Orpah, the widows of her sons, to each return to her mother's home so they might find security, food, and shelter—all of the things she would not be able to provide for them. Orpah listened to Naomi, and after weeping with her and kissing her, she returned to her family. But Ruth clung to her husband's mother and spoke the words of that beautiful promise, *"Entreat me not to leave you..."*

Ruth left her home, her family, and the way of life she had always known. She turned her back completely on her past and promised to go with Naomi even to the point of death. Ruth demonstrated unfaltering loyalty to her mother-in-law. Most importantly, she accepted the God of Naomi as her God. Ruth's loving commitment to Naomi would change the course of her life and would, ultimately, change the course of history.

Boaz and Ruth

Ruth traveled to Bethlehem with Naomi. They arrived at the beginning of the barley harvest, and Ruth immediately began to make plans for their survival. For Ruth, as a Moabite woman, it was a new city, with new people and new customs. She asked Naomi if she could go to a field and glean heads of grain from behind the harvesters. It had been commanded by God that landowners leave anything dropped or not picked up by the harvesters so the poor and the strangers in the land could have a supply of food (Lev. 19:9-10). The Bible says Ruth *happened* to go to the part of the field that was owned by a man named Boaz, a relative of Naomi's late husband, Elimelech.

When Boaz went to check on his reapers, he took notice of Ruth and asked about her. After learning about her devotion to Naomi, Boaz made her a generous offer. He invited her to continue gleaning in his field. There, she would have protection and provision. He even requested that his servants allow her to glean among the sheaves and that they let grain purposely fall from the bundles so she might have more to glean. Boaz had said to Ruth, *"The Lord repay your work, and a full reward be given you by the Lord God of Israel, under whose wings you have come for refuge"* (Ruth 2:12). God was certainly watching over Ruth. She didn't just *happen* to come to the field of Boaz. She came to his field by the providence of God.

When Ruth returned home that evening she told Naomi about Boaz. Naomi was overjoyed! She explained to Ruth how they were related to Boaz and encouraged her to remain in his field.

Boaz, Ruth, and Naomi each worked for the good of another. Cooperation in action! Ruth helped Naomi. Boaz helped Ruth. Naomi helped Ruth. Love is abounding in this story.

Naomi wanted to be sure that Ruth would be cared for and believed that Boaz, as a relative of her husband, could be her kinsmen-redeemer. Ruth followed the advice of her mother-in-law, and one night when Boaz lay down to sleep on the threshing floor, Ruth walked softly to him, uncovered his feet, and lay down. At midnight he woke up and saw her. "Who are you?" he asked.

"I am your servant Ruth," she answered. "Take me under your wing for you are a close relative."

Boaz again showed kindness to Ruth. He said to her, "And now my daughter, do not fear, I will do for you all that you request, for all the people of my town know that you are a virtuous woman" (Ruth 3:11). There was just one problem. There was another man, an even closer relative, who would have the first right to buy Elimelech's land and marry Ruth. As a good and honest man, Boaz would have to give that relative the opportunity to be the kinsman-redeemer.

In the end, the closer relative declined and Boaz bought all that had been Elimelech's. He took Ruth to be his wife, and they would later become the grandparents of a shepherd boy named David and ancestors of the Messiah. Theirs was a lineage of love.

God and His People

The story of Ruth is a beautiful metaphor for the love that God has for his people. It parallels his relationship with Israel, and on a broader scale, his relationship with you and me.

People may not have thought much about Ruth. She was a foreigner from a pagan country. She was a widow with no money, and she lived with her widowed mother-in-law. It appeared that she had little to offer. Her situation was pretty hopeless. But that's not what God saw! He saw her value. He saw her importance. He had a role for her to fill in his plan for all of mankind, and he worked the events of her life together for good. His Son, Jesus, would be her descendant, and her name would be remembered for eternity.

God uses unremarkable people to carry out his remarkable plans. He calls on the weak, the timid, and the unimpressive to accomplish his will for his glory. We see it time again in Scripture through the stories of David, Gideon, Esther, Tamar, Rahab, Paul, John Mark, and so many others.

Ruth needed a redeemer. She was poor and broken. She had lost everything. Boaz came into her life and cared for her, loved her, and saved her.

We needed a Redeemer. Just like Ruth, we were broken and lost. Sin had robbed us of everything. We were hopeless. But Jesus came to this world because he cares for us and loves us. He redeemed us and rescued us from sin. Jesus is our Boaz. Our Kinsman, our Redeemer, and our Bridegroom. Isaiah the prophet wrote, *"For your Maker is your husband, the Lord of hosts*

IN HIS STEPS

Jesus came to this world to live as a man because of love. He lived a sinless life because of love. He suffered on the cross because of love. He lives again because of love. Love is the motivation behind our salvation. Our Savior, Jesus Christ, IS love by his very nature.

"By this we know_____, because He laid down His_____ for us. And we also ought to lay down our _____ for the brethren" (1 John 13:16).

is His name; and your Redeemer is the Holy One of Israel; He is called the God of the whole earth" (Isaiah 54:5).

OUR DAILY WALK

As you are going about each day, you are creating an image of Christ to others by the way that you live. Through your love, you are painting of picture of Jesus to the world. Before you pick up your spiritual paintbrush, ask yourself this question, *"Why do I love Jesus?"* This will provide you with artistic inspiration as you begin painting.

I've asked myself that question before, *"Why do I love Jesus?"* and it's not something that I struggle to answer. It's not a question that requires me to disappear under a deluge of books and commentaries in order to reach a conclusion, and it's not something I couldn't explain in a simple way to a young child. What's difficult about this question is that it deserves so much more than a quick thought and a bullet point list.

To ask the question *"Why do I love Jesus?"* is to consider a collection of beautiful, extraordinary, incomprehensible, and life-changing truths. These truths are effectual, not only personally, but in my relationship with the world around me. In other words, when I think about the reasons I have for loving Jesus, it should change *everything*. It should change the way I think, the way I react, the way I speak, the way I treat people, and the way I live out my day to day life in general.

The sum of my reasons for loving Jesus is this: *He loves me.*

And that reason permeates into every facet of my life and influences all that I say and do. As I walk through my day, I walk in love because Jesus showed me kindness and mercy. I walk in love because Jesus suffered for me. I walk in love because Jesus' blood cleanses me continually of my sin. I walk in love because Jesus is advocating for me in Heaven. I walk in love because Jesus gave me hope.

When I think about why I love Jesus, I am reminded of the gracious ways he has shown his love for me. Then I pick up my paintbrush and begin painting through my words, and my actions, and my attitude toward others. I pray that the picture that I am painting for people is one that depicts the unconditional, unending love of Jesus.

Remember this as you live day to day. *What picture am I painting of Jesus?*

STRENGTH

What do you think is the greatest characteristic of love?

In what ways do you show love for your spouse? Your family? Your co-workers? How about the lost, the lonely, and the hurting?

How do you show compassion? How has someone been compassionate toward you?

TRIALS

We are commanded to love our enemies (Matthew 5:44). How do you love the unlovable? How do we express that love?

The love that we read about in the Bible sometimes clashes with the world's definition of love. How does society view love? How can we demonstrate the love of Jesus when we disagree with someone's definition of love?

To share the Truth is an expression of love. What challenges does that present in our world today?

ENCOURAGEMENT

Think about the kind of picture you want to paint. If you could paint a picture of Jesus for the world, what would be in it? What would it look like?

You may have seen this exercise before, but I thought I would include it here because it's a wonderful reminder of the type of people we should strive to be: *people who reflect love*. The following verses are taken from 1 Corinthians 13, commonly referred to as "The Love Chapter" of the Bible. Together these verses provide a description of love. I have taken out the word "love" and replaced it with a blank line. Write your name on each of those blank lines and then read the text again.

"_____ suffers long and is kind; _____
does not envy; _____ does not parade herself, is not puffed
up; does not behave rudely, does not seek her own, is not provoked, thinks no
evil; does not rejoice in iniquity, but rejoices in the truth; bears all things, believes all things, hopes all things, endures all things" (1 Corinthians 13:4-7).

This should define who we are as Christians! This is what we want to reflect
to the world!

PRAYER

*Loving Father, you have provided me with everything. You have given me life
and surrounded me with blessings. You have forgiven me, removed my sin,
and offered me hope. You have loved me and taken care of me when I have
done nothing to deserve your mercy or grace. Thank you, God, for choosing me
and wanting me to be your child.*

*I want to love like you. I want to have a heart that seeks the highest good for
others. Please work in me and through me that I might develop that kind of a
heart. Lead me to people who desperately need to come to know you and help
me show them your love.*

*Help me to love the unlovable, forgive the unforgiveable, teach the unteachable,
and touch the untouchable. Grow within me a spirit of compassion, caring,
and commitment.*

Thank you for Jesus, your greatest gift of love.

In his name I pray, Amen

WALK WITH THE DOC

Walking tip: Walk with others

Time is precious when there is less of it to waste. Time dedicated to walking can be used for the dual purpose of sharing time with others. It is the perfect means of creating and sustaining relationships. Forty minutes to an hour of uninterrupted time is hard to come by these days. Sharing the walking experience can be a source of reciprocal encouragement. Participating in 5 and 10k events in the community can be a rewarding experience. Walking in a half marathon with thousands of others of like-mind can be downright exciting when shared with friends and family. Parents and grandparents, walk with your children and grandchildren, and often. You'll be surprised how receptive they'll be. Time, precious time, share it when you can, on and off the trail.

TAKE ACTION!

Add others to your walk and walk when you're with others! If you are having a meeting at work, make it a walking meeting. If you're planning a get together with family, incorporate some type of physical activity. Sign up for a 5k or 10k with your friends. Walking with others is fun, and it also provides built in accountability.

Walk with someone you love. Talk, share, laugh, recall, and dream together as you go. The time is invaluable, and the memories are irreplaceable!

CHAPTER TWELVE
WHEN NO ONE IS LOOKING
Walk with Integrity

"Better is the poor who walks in his integrity than one perverse in his ways though he be rich" (Proverbs 28:6).

*I*f you are a nurse, or ever decide to become a nurse, you will know (or will soon find out) that your ability to perform a complete and accurate nursing assessment is of paramount importance. It is one of the first lessons you will learn as a nursing student, and it's a skill that you will use regularly and will continue to sharpen throughout your nursing career. The "Head-to-Toe Assessment" has kept many a student up all night reciting cranial nerves and characterizing lung sounds before the practical demonstration with an instructor.

One aspect of the nursing assessment involves the skin. You take into consideration skin color, temperature, texture, and moisture. As part of the assessment, an evaluation is made of the skin's integrity to determine whether the skin is whole, undamaged, and intact. You are specifically assessing for any broken areas or potential breakdown. You are inspecting the skin for the presence of skin tears, blisters, wounds, and pressure sores. When you are taking care of a patient in the hospital, this assessment is performed regularly—at least once a shift and more often if the patient already has issues with their skin or if they are at high risk for developing problems.

You might be wondering why the skin is given so much attention?! The skin is the body's largest organ and one of its first lines of defense when it comes to infection. It keeps the body's temperature regulated, protects the inner organs, provides electrolyte balance, and allows us to experience sensations such as pain, heat, cold, and touch. With the loss of integrity, skin becomes thinner, loses its elasticity, takes longer to heal, and is not able to perform its important job functions. There are things that you can do in order to maintain skin integrity. First, you have to keep moving! Too much time in one place is not good for the skin. If your job requires you to sit for long periods of time, remember to stand up and stretch, move around for a bit, and change positions. Next, you should have a skin care regimen in place that includes cleansing, drying, and moisturizing. You also should keep your skin protected when you're in the sun. And it is always of great importance that you remain hydrated and pay special attention to your nutrition requirements. All of these things will help keep your skin strong, healthy, and whole.

The integrity of the skin can teach us something meaningful about the integrity of a Christian. The two are relative in a variety of ways. When it comes to a follower of Jesus, an evaluation of her life should reveal integrity that is intact. The evidence can be found in her truthfulness, her sameness, and her wholeness.

Truthfulness

Conforming to the mind, will, character, glory, and being of God.

The integrity of a patient's skin can give you a glimpse into the reality of her daily physical life. An assessment that reveals areas of redness, pain, or wounds, might indicate a problem related to her mobility or nutritional status. Even more, it could lead to questions about her living conditions and support systems. Skin integrity can disclose the truth about much deeper issues related to a person's wellness.

In much the same way, our integrity as Christians is the manifestation of the truth by which we live. Truth, by biblical definition, is God. Truth is his Word and the way in which he leads. Truth is Jesus and the Spirit. Living a life of truthfulness is living a life that is in harmony with God and his will. When we live in that way, we demonstrate integrity.

The book of Ezra gives us helpful instructions on how we can reflect the truth in our lives. In Ezra 7:10 we read, *"For Ezra had prepared his heart to seek the Law of the Lord, and to do it, and to teach statutes and ordinances in Israel."* Notice these four ways Ezra shows us we should handle the Truth:

- Prepare your heart – Set your heart on living for the Truth. Make the decision.
- Seek the Law of the Lord – God's Word is Truth. Study it, loyally.
- Then do it – Be obedient. This is Truth in action!
- And teach it – Share the Truth with others.

When we follow the example of Ezra, our lives will reflect the integrity that comes from living a life of truthfulness.

Sameness

Being exactly who you say you are.

A skin assessment requires a complete head to toe exam. No areas of skin are left unobserved. If I evaluate the anterior surface of a patient's skin, but I never turn him over to evaluate the posterior side, I would not have a complete picture of his skin condition. It might appear healthy and intact from the front, but if there is a Stage IV pressure ulcer on the back of his right heel, it would not be correct to say that he has good skin integrity.

Our integrity as Christians has to have the element of uniformity. What we say and how we live should tell the same story regardless of our company and our circumstance. We are the same everywhere, all of the time. Whether it's Sunday morning when we're gathered for worship, or Monday morning at our job, or throughout our weekend get-a-way, *we are the same.* Whether we are with our spouse, our children, our co-workers, our Bible study group, or strangers out in public, *we are the same.* Whether asked to give testimony of our faith at a devotional of fellow Christians or in a situation that might result in persecution, *we are the same.*

Integrity is remaining committed to our faith, no matter the consequence. The quality of sameness is one that our Savior possesses. Hebrews 13:8 says, *"Jesus Christ is the same yesterday, today, and forever."* Jesus is the picture of integrity because we can count on him to never, ever change.

Wholeness

Having perfect unity of the body, mind, and spirit.

The skin is one facet of the marvelous, miraculous creation that is the human body. It has a vital role in our health and the overall state of wellness. When the skin is whole, or unbroken, it's doing its part to keep the rest of the body in good working order. When the skin is intact, infection has one less mode of entry, the balance of electrolytes and water is better maintained, and our body temperature can be well maintained. The wholeness of the skin positively influences the entire body.

Integrity in the life of the Christian affects every aspect of our being. When we practice integrity, we bring our body, mind, and spirit into a state of unity. We strive for perfection, or completeness, in this area, but the Bible tells us that we are a work in progress. We are being transformed into the image of Jesus Christ with ever increasing glory (2 Corinthians 3:18) until the day he comes again and we attain the full measure of his likeness (Ephesians 4:13; 1 John 3:2). What a day that will be!

Our prayer should be like the prayer of Paul for the Thessalonians, *"Now may the God of peace Himself sanctify you completely; and may your whole spirit, soul, and body, be preserved blameless at the coming of our Lord Jesus Christ. He who calls you is faithful, who also will do it"* (1 Thessalonians 5:23). We do our part by living a life of integrity and God will continue his good work until Jesus returns (Philippians 1:6).

As with the skin, the integrity of a Christian helps to protect the inner man. It wards off sin that attempts to infect our bodies and keeps our spirits regulated regardless of the heat or pain of a situation. It helps us to experience the sensations of love, courage, and trust. It requires continual assessment so that we can be aware of any dangers of breakdown. Integrity is something we work to maintain everyday so that it will remain strong, healthy, and whole.

A WALKING WARRIOR

"...but they could find no charge or fault, because he was faithful; nor was there any error or fault found in him" (Daniel 6:4).

When I began to choose men and women from the Bible for the "Walking Warrior" section of each chapter of this book, I knew that I would use Daniel somewhere. *But where?* Walking in the ways of the Lord, humbly, carefully, faithfully, uprightly, with wise men…all of these describe the character of the man called Daniel. Then came this chapter: *Integrity*. And I knew this is where his story would shine. He drew lines that would not be crossed. He made promises that would not be broken. He was *always* the same: he *always* chose God over man.

I like the definition of integrity that is found on the website vocabulary.com: "Having integrity means doing the right thing in a reliable way. It's a personality trait that we admire, since it means a person has a moral compass that doesn't waver. It literally means having 'wholeness' of character, just as an integer is a 'whole number' with no fractions." I think that is the perfect description of Daniel: unwavering and undivided.

Five "C's" of Daniel's Character

CONVICTED – Daniel held firmly to his belief in God, and it was obvious by the way that he lived. In other words, his behavior reflected his belief. The conviction of his heart became the commitment of his life. We see this in the first chapter of Daniel, when he is still young and has been brought to serve in the palace of King Nebuchadnezzar. He took a stand when it came to the food and drink provided by the Babylonian king knowing that it was unclean and unholy. In Daniel 1:6 it says, *"But Daniel purposed in his heart that he would not defile himself with the portion of the king's delicacies, nor with the wine which he drank; therefore, he requested of the chief of the eunuchs that he might not defile himself."*

The phrase "purposed in his heart" is translated in other versions as "resolved," "determined," and "made up his mind." These words give a clear indication that Daniel took a strong stand that was in keeping with his faith. We find Daniel taking another strong stand a few chapters later when he ignores the law signed by King Darius forbidding him to pray to God for a period of thirty days. He took a strong stand every time he was called on to interpret dreams, speaking the truth rather than telling powerful men what they wanted to hear. Daniel lived what he believed. Never compromising; never apologizing; always faithful.

COMPASSIONATE – I picked this word to describe Daniel because of the kindness he showed others throughout his life, even his enemies. He didn't waver when it came to his beliefs and defended them in such a way that earned him the respect of those who opposed him. He found favor with the chief of the eunuchs in King Nebuchadnezzar's court (Daniel 1:8) and was distinguished above the governors and officials because of his excellent spirit (Daniel 6:3). Daniel was well liked, and I believe from the examples we have in Scripture, it was in part because of the compassion he showed others without discrimination.

- He did not forget his faithful friends when he was receiving honor (Daniel 2:49).
- He understood the grim reality behind Nebuchadnezzar's dream and wished that the vision was concerning the king's enemies and not the king himself (Daniel 4:20).
- He encouraged the king to be merciful to the poor (Daniel 4:27).
- He refused the gifts and rewards that the king offered in exchange for interpreting his dream (Daniel 5:17).
- He prayed for his people. He repented on their behalf and asked for their forgiveness (Daniel 9).
- He never criticized the people who tried to bring him down.
- He demonstrated respect for those in leadership positions.

Daniel's reputation preceded him throughout his life. People knew he was a man of God, and they could always be sure of where his loyalties lay. But, they could also count on his compassion. In Daniel 5:11, the queen described Daniel to King Belshazzar as a man "in whom is the Spirit of the Holy God." With the Spirit active in his life, we can be sure that Daniel was not only faithful, but also kind and good.

CONSISTENT – From the days of his youth to old age, Daniel loved and obeyed God. Day or night, good or bad, in peace or in threat of danger, Daniel did what was right. He didn't change to please man; he consistently focused on pleasing God. If you ask most people for a definition of integrity, they might tell you something like this, "Integrity is doing the right thing even when no one is watching." That's a wonderful way to describe it! You do what's right regardless of who you're with, where you are, and how you feel. If you live by the Truth and the Truth never changes, then neither does your behavior when it comes to living it out in your daily life.

Earlier I mentioned the law that forbade prayer for thirty days. Listen to the words we read in Daniel 6:10, *"Now when Daniel knew that the writing was signed, he went home. And in his upper room, with his window open toward Jerusalem, he knelt down on his knees three times that day, and prayed and gave thanks before his God, as was his custom since early days."*

Daniel didn't change. He knew that the decree was passed, but he kept on doing what he'd always been doing because it was the right thing to do. He could have submitted to the law, waited for the thirty days to pass, and then resumed his prayer life. He could have prayed in secret, behind a closed window. Instead, he remained true to his values and prayed the same way he had been praying all along.

COMPLETELY TRUSTED – Daniel didn't cower when confronted with opposition; instead he faced his enemies and challenges with courage and strength, qualities that resulted from his complete trust in God. As penalty for praying to God in violation of the law, Daniel was thrown into a den of lions (Daniel 6:16-17). The next morning when the mouth of the den was unsealed, the Bible says, *"So Daniel was taken up out of the den, and no injury whatever was found on him, because he believed in his God"* (Daniel 6:23).

Daniel believed God would save him, and God did. He didn't fear man. He lived the words of Jesus found in Matthew 10:28, *"And do not fear those who kill the body but cannot kill the soul. But rather fear Him who is able to destroy both soul and body in hell."* Daniel's name means, "God my judge," and I believe that phrase was his mantra. "Whatever happens in this life, God is my judge."

Daniel didn't concern himself with the consequences handed down to him from man. He did what was right and trusted that God would take care of him. He knew that, ultimately, only God's judgment matters.

He trusted God, and he prospered! (Daniel 1:17, 20; Daniel 2:48; Daniel 5:10-12; Daniel 5:29; Daniel 6:28; Daniel 12:13).

COMMENDED GLORY TO GOD – Daniel recognized that his abilities and his wisdom came from God, and he glorified God for those good gifts. In Daniel 2, God reveals to Daniel the meaning of King Nebuchadnezzar's dream and in verse 23 as part of his prayer of thanksgiving Daniel says, *"I thank You* and praise You, O God of my fathers; You have given me wisdom and might, and have now made known to me what I asked of You, for You have made known to us the king's demand." How often do we humbly thank God for the talents he has given us?

A few verses later, when the king asks Daniel if he is able to interpret his dream, Daniel takes no credit for himself and instead tells the king, "But there is a God in Heaven who reveals secrets, and He has made known to King Nebuchadnezzar what will be in the latter days." How often, when asked about our gifts and abilities, do we give the glory to God? Daniel lived his life as an instrument for God's glory.

Daniel's life calls out from the pages of the Old Testament confirming the words spoken by Paul to Timothy, "all who desire to live godly in Christ Jesus will suffer persecution" (2 Timothy 2:12).

Through his conviction, compassion, consistency, complete trust, and commending glory to God, Daniel continues to teach us what it means to walk in integrity. His book closes with these words: "But you, go your way till the end; for you shall rest, and will arise to your inheritance at the end of these days" (Daniel 12:13). We can know that the good man Daniel has received his reward.

IN HIS STEPS

The way Jesus lived told the story of Christianity: God's perfect Son left Heaven to walk among men and die a cruel death as a young teacher and healer who only showed love and kindness to the world. He always did what was right. He *always* spoke the truth.

"Who committed no _____, nor was _____ found in His mouth" (1 Peter 2:22).

OUR DAILY WALK

As you walk through each day, how are you representing Christianity to the people around you? Do your actions, your attitude, and the things you say, reflect the goodness of Christ and the joy you have because of what he's done for you? Do people see that there is something different about you? I read somewhere that "your life will demonstrate to the people around you whether Christianity is true or false." That's a pretty powerful statement; one that takes serious consideration. Do people see you as someone who says one thing but does another? Does your life confirm the Truth of the Gospel? It will if you live by the Spirit according to the Word!

Someone is always watching you. Remember that. Little eyes, older eyes, lost eyes, searching eyes, struggling eyes—people are looking at you and are influenced by what they see you do. They notice how you handle conflicts, how you defend your faith, how you treat others, how you live when you think no one is paying attention. Be the heroine in the movie who makes the right choice when she comes to a moral fork in the road. She thinks as she faces her challenge, "*Do I do what's easy even though it's wrong, or do I do what's right even though it might be difficult?*" She chooses to do what's right, hope is restored, and the audience breaks out in applause! Be her. Be the one to take a stand for the Truth when everyone else is compromising, backsliding, and excusing their way out of it.

Think about the conviction of Daniel. Think about his consistency and compassion. Think about how he completely trusted in God and always gave God the glory for the successes in his life. Be a Daniel—a true person of integrity!

Decide, at the beginning of the day, that you will do the right thing. Purpose in your heart. Plan to choose God over man—Every. Single. Time. Make up your mind that for today you will do what you *should* do before those things that you might really *want* to do. This will mean putting your spiritual self first, and sometimes our fleshly self doesn't make that too easy. But you can do it! "*Set your mind on things above...*"

Don't make promises you can't keep. Don't say one thing and then do another. Don't change your stand depending on the room you're in or the company you're keeping.

Do be the kind of friend to Jesus that he is to you. Be truthful. Be the same. Be whole.

STRENGTH

How does walking in integrity set you apart from the world?

Describe how truthfulness, sameness, and wholeness characterize a person of integrity.

Truthfulness –

Sameness –

Wholeness –

Daniel is described in Scripture as having an "excellent spirit." What does it mean to have an excellent spirit?

TRIALS

How can walking in integrity be costly?

How does a person of integrity prepare for trials?

How does someone improve in this area? In other words, how can someone become better at living a life of integrity?

ENCOURAGEMENT

Send a note to a young person and tell him about something good you saw him do when he thought no one was watching! This can be a message sent through Facebook or a text that you can send by phone. Just contact a young person and let her know that her goodness does not go unnoticed. This means more to our young friends than we realize.

You might also want to share the following poem if you have the opportunity. We talk about who our "friends" are on social media, and we share things and say things that we only want our friends to see and hear; but, Jesus is our friend in the real world *and* the virtual world. We need to be sure that what we post, or tweet, or snap is something we would share with him, too. Who we are on social media should reflect who we are as Christians.

Innergram

Behind each posted picture,
behind every blog you read,
behind each status update,
behind every single "tweet,"

There stands a man or woman—
maybe young or maybe old
you may not see him face-to-face,
but each one has a soul.

They may be worlds apart,
separated by a screen,
but each has been created
in the image of the King.

Which one follows Jesus?
Which one walks the Narrow Way?
Can others tell that YOU do,
by the virtual things YOU say?

When friends read your profile,
or the laundry that you've aired,
do they know that you're a Christian
by the message that you've shared?

Just like in the real world,
your goal on-line should be the same,
Be sure that all you say and do
brings glory to His name.

Take a look inside yourself
and before you "post" or "send,"
Remember no matter where you are,
Jesus is your *friend*.

by Lori Boyd

PRAYER

Dear Heavenly Father, I thank you for being the same yesterday, today, and tomorrow. I thank you for being true to your promises. I thank you for loving me when I am faithful and when I fall.

I pray to walk with integrity every day. Help me to be convicted, compassionate, and consistent in the way I live my life. Help me to completely trust you in my losses and to commend glory to you in my triumphs.

Forgive me when I allow myself to be influenced by the world around me, and give me the strength I need to stand up for what I believe no matter what con-

sequence I might receive.

Develop an excellent spirit in me, like Daniel.

In Jesus' Name, Amen

WALK WITH THE DOC

Walking tip: Walking can improve your self-esteem

Take steps to feel better about yourself. So often folks just "let themselves go." Basically it is an issue of ill-placed priorities and poor stewardship. Maintaining a healthy, fit body and overall sense of well-being takes time and effort. Simply knowing that you're doing the right thing builds self-esteem. "Do you not know that your body is a temple of the Holy Spirit, who is within you...and that you are not your own?" (1 Corinthians 6:19-20). That scripture alone is reason enough to become a responsible steward. It is the Lord's will. There is little doubt that by pursuing an active walking program you will in time notice considerable improvement in your health, fitness, appearance, and overall self-esteem.

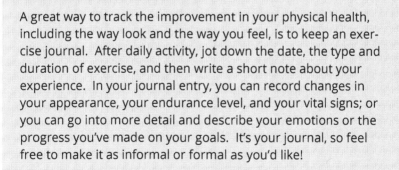

TAKE ACTION!

A great way to track the improvement in your physical health, including the way look and the way you feel, is to keep an exercise journal. After daily activity, jot down the date, the type and duration of exercise, and then write a short note about your experience. In your journal entry, you can record changes in your appearance, your endurance level, and your vital signs; or you can go into more detail and describe your emotions or the progress you've made on your goals. It's your journal, so feel free to make it as informal or formal as you'd like!

CHAPTER THIRTEEN
BE GOOD, DO GOOD
Walk in Good Works

"For we are His workmanship, created in Christ Jesus for good works, which God prepared beforehand that we should walk in them" (Ephesians 2:10).

*E*very moment of every day is an opportunity to do something good for someone else. According to the verse above, it's why we were created. The idea of doing a nice thing for someone every now and then (good deed….check!) needs to be replaced with the idea that our entire lives should be a gift to others in an on-going, never-ending, this-is-who-I-am, kind of way. As God's child and Christ's aroma I should be busy impacting the world for good to the degree that the world takes notice. And my goal? *Always* that God will be glorified.

To talk more about good works and how we should live them and make them a part of our wilderness journey, I'm going to need the help of a fish, a Frisbee, a flashback, a fingerprint, and a flower.

A Fish

Dr. Pepper came into our lives in the summer of 2012. We had attended the Vacation Bible School at a little congregation southeast of Woodbury, Tennessee and on the last night, Briggs was given a special "take-home" gift. Every kid in his class was given a goldfish. *A real one.* Not a little baggy of snack cracker goldfish, but a completely alive, gill-bearing, aquatic animal. The fish came in a little glass bowl with lots of colorful rocks…and no instructions.

On the way home that night, Briggs named his fish "Dr. Pepper." I can't remember for the life of me how Briggs came up with that name, but I do remember that we all laughed and thought it was perfect! Dr. Pepper was then officially considered part of the Boyd family, along with Mole and One Third, our two guinea pigs, and Pearl, our dog.

As it turned out, we had some things to learn about owning a goldfish. After the first couple of days, Dr. Pepper did not seem to be thriving. We cleaned his bowl, we cleaned his rocks, and we fed him plenty, but nothing helped. I launched into some intense goldfish research on the computer and learned that goldfish cannot live in small, unfiltered bowls of water. I had no idea! I've seen goldfish sold in little glass bowls in pet shops my entire life and always assumed that's where they stay! Since Dr. Pepper appeared unwell, and time was of the essence, we had to take drastic life-saving measures.

We activated "Operation Goldfish Rescue" and headed to my parents' house to release Dr. Pepper into their well-maintained koi pond. There he could be free and swim in filtered happiness. It was a thirty-minute drive and a race with time. About half-way there, Evie, who was holding the bowl in the backseat, called out, "We better hurry! Dr. Pepper just fainted!"

Well, I knew that Dr. Pepper had experienced more than a lapse in consciousness, but as I looked back at the faces of my three animal-loving children, I knew that we had to see this mission through to the end. I explained that the "fainting" was not a good sign, but that we would still do our very best to help him. When we got to Mom and Dad's, the kids jumped out of the car and ran to the pond. They released Dr. Pepper into the water, but our fears were confirmed—it was too late.

Dr. Pepper was buried in my Mom's garden after we said some nice things about the fish we had known for just a couple of days. I'm realizing as I write this down, that this is an awfully sad sounding story, but there is a lesson hidden here that is very important when it comes to good works:

The good work you do for someone over something that seems quite insignificant can have grand and enduring effects. What I hope that my children learned from Dr. Pepper is that nothing—and no one—is too small for the investment of your time and attention. This story is about a fish, but think about it in terms of a person who needs help. How far do you go? How much time do you give?

We recognized that our goldfish had a need. We researched, we planned, and we took time to help him. He was a *fish*. There are people everywhere who are gasping for air in an unfiltered world. Are we taking the time to get them what they need? It might be a lost sinner, or a struggling Christian; whoever it is, they need our time and attention.

Good works can involve giving your time.

A Frisbee

When Dad was working on his residency in ophthalmology at Duke University, he spent some time in Africa studying tropical eye diseases. After completing that program Dad would occasionally return to Africa to participate in medical mission work. I remember watching him pack his suitcase and listening to his stories about the people and places he would see. Before Dad left he would let me and my sisters collect some toys and clothes to send with him on his trip, and he would hand them out to children in the villages he visited.

Before one particular trip, my sisters and I gave Dad a Frisbee. He thought it would be something the kids would really enjoy, so he ended up taking a bag full of them. The Frisbee didn't cross our minds again until Dad came home. When he did, he sat down with us and told us exactly what had become of our toy.

The children in one of the villages of Tanzania had never seen anything like a Frisbee. They held it, felt it, and turned it over and over in their hands. They threw it to each other, and they rolled it on its side like a wheel. They loved their new toy. But that wasn't all!

The adults were excited about the Frisbee, too! The women dipped it into the river to scoop up water and used it as a bowl for serving food. The men would hold the Frisbee between their knees and beat it like a drum. The Frisbee was loved and appreciated by everyone in the village.

Jenny, Julia, and I sat and listened to Dad talk about how much joy came from a simple, plastic toy. I clearly recall the happy feeling that grew from deep down inside my six-year-old self. I closed my eyes and could see that bright pink Frisbee being passed from hand to hand, and I felt like I'd done something good.

Good works can involve giving your things.

A Flashback

When my daughter Kate was six years old she met an elderly couple at our congregation. It took Kate no time at all to recognize that the Carpenters were special people, and she fell into a sweet friendship with them. Every time we came together for worship, Kate would find Mr. and Mrs. Carpenter, hug their necks, and talk to them about everything in the world she was doing. They loved Kate and were always so attentive to her when she came to visit with them. That went on for years.

One day, Kate received a letter in the mail from Mr. Carpenter. I wondered what it could have been for—it wasn't her birthday and nothing significant had happened lately to require congratulations. I could hardly wait for Kate to get home from school to open it!

She was thrilled to have been sent a letter. She tore it open with eager little hands and wide-open eyes. Inside there was a notecard with a long hand-written message as well as a faded black and white photograph. The picture was of Mr. and Mrs. Carpenter when they were young and had just started dating. Mr. Carpenter had written out the story about how he and Mrs. Carpenter had met and fallen in love. He described all of it to Kate. He told her where they were living, what year it was, where they went, and what his sweetheart looked like.

Kate read every word. It meant the world to her. He had shared their life story with her, and it made her feel important. It made her feel like she mattered to them, not just as a sweet little girl who gave good hugs, but as a dear friend. She held that notecard with her eight-year-old hands reading the words written by a friend who was 90 years her senior, and felt very special. I am forever grateful to Mr. Carpenter and that good work that he did. He gave my Kate a valuable gift.

Good works can involve sharing your life.

A Fingerprint

I keep everything. I have a very hard time throwing anything away because I'm pretty sure that as soon as I do, I'll regret it and desperately want it back. Sometimes I feel bad about stockpiling, but one thing I never think twice about is saving every piece of artwork that was made with my children's fingerprints.

I have a beautiful treasure of fingerprint memorabilia: ghosts, flower petals, turkeys, and Santa Claus faces. I have drawings of fingerprint faces, fingerprint poems, and fingerprint bookmarks. I have a collection of papers and do-dads that bear the marks of fingers and thumbs that I wouldn't trade for all of the money in the world. *Why?* Because they've been literally touched by the three little people who I love so intensely.

Their fingerprint presents are like receiving a small piece of who they are. It's as if they've taken a bit of themselves and with a touch of ink or a brush of paint imprinted it onto paper and presented me with a gift of love to hold on to forever. And you bet I will. I will hold onto those fingerprint reindeer even if it means gluing on the red nose (again) every Christmas for the next fifty years!

There is something extra special about a gift made with hands. It's a gift that represents the heart of the giver. It's a gift that involves time and effort. These types of gifts are meaningful because they are deeply personal (to the getter and the giver) and running over with love.

Good works can involve giving yourself.

A Flower

My husband knows how much I love fresh flowers. He keeps my kitchen counter looking pretty with bright bouquets. When he makes a run to the store, he will often grab some flowers for me while he's there if he knows my vase is empty or in need of refreshing. I love that he knows they make me happy and so he keeps them coming! He's wonderful like that.

My son has seen Sam bring me flowers for years. Now, when they go to the store together, Briggs will go into the floral section and want to pick out the bouquet to bring home. The first time Briggs came back from the store with flowers, he brought them straight to me and dropped down on his knee. Then, with all the charm in his little body and a smolder that rivals Flynn Rider's in *Tangled*, he held up the flowers and sweetly asked, "Will you be my mother?"

A thousand times "yes!" I wrapped my arms around Briggs and held him tight. Such a thoughtful boy who's learning acts of kindness just by watching his Dad.

Those two men in my life bring me flowers to show me that they care about me. They sure know how to fill up my heart. I don't really *need* the bouquets, but I love that they love me enough to notice when my vase needs new residents.

Good works can involve giving your love.

A WALKING WARRIOR

Dorcas lived in Joppa, a port city located on the Mediterranean coast. She is described as being a disciple (and in that one word there is a deeply important message), but we aren't told much more about this woman who has been remembered forever in Scripture for the valuable lessons taught through her life. We don't know how old she was, we don't know about her family, and we don't know if she was rich or poor, if she was married or not. However, we do know that she was loved and that her death broke the hearts of many people who had been touched by her kindness.

We all know a Dorcas—a "woman full of good works and charitable deeds." She blesses the lives of others in simple and quiet ways, never for her own glory, but simply because she enjoys helping people. She personifies Ephesians 2:10 and fulfills her created purpose. Read the story of Dorcas found in Acts 9:36-43 and let's see what she continues to teach us from the pages of the Bible.

A Disciple of Christ

The first lesson we learn from Dorcas is that she was a disciple. What does that mean? What does that tell us specifically about this woman? The Greek word for "disciple" in this context is *mathetria* and literally means a "female pupil." Discipleship in the New Testament carried with it the idea of learning or making other learners. The disciples of Jesus sat and learned from him as their Rabbi, and he didn't accept a select number of students—he accepted any who would come! When he traveled, they traveled with him, and so his disciples were also referred to as "followers."

Being a disciple doesn't mean just sitting at the feet of Jesus, nodding your head in agreement, and then walking away unchanged. It means leaving where you are and following him. It means denying everything else and living differently. Being his disciple means you adopt the way that he looked at the world, you learn from him, you apply his teachings to your life, you are changed by him, and then you bring other people to him. The church needs faithful disciples of Jesus! To give you an idea of how important this concept is: the word "disciple" is used 264 times in the New Testament.

Think for a moment about the disciples of Jesus in the first century. Those men and women followed their Teacher down the streets of Judea, along the coast, and over mountains. When he left them to return to Heaven, they continued to take his message into cities and country sides. They were devout students who were dedicated to teaching others about Jesus. I believe that if we begin to see ourselves as disciples of Christ, learners and followers of him, we could change the world! We could bring more souls into the church by living out the Gospel message in our daily lives and then inviting people to learn more about God's plan of redemption. This world so desperately needs Jesus!

Dorcas was a disciple—a disciple who did nice things for people! Take a look at how the Scriptures in our text describe the good works that she did.

Full, Alone, Small, Memorable, and Present

1. She was *full* of good works and charitable deeds (v. 36). The New American Standard Version says that she was *"abounding with deeds of kindness and charity which she continually did."* Dorcas didn't do good works every now and then—she was abounding with them! In other words, she spent a lot of her time doing good things for people. In fact, she did them "continually." She reminds me of the description that Peter gives of Jesus in the next chapter, as someone who "went about doing good" (Acts 10:38). It's who Jesus was and what he did. As Christians, it should be who we are and what we do.

2. She did the works *on her own* (v. 36). At the end of verse 36 there are three words that give us some insight on the good works of Dor-

cas: *"which she did."* The good works that she did were not a collective effort. *She* did them. The text doesn't say that she worked with a small group or that she was a part of a congregational service project; it refers to her works and deeds as something *she* did. This is not to discount the value or importance of working together to provide for others; but it does beg the question, "What are you and I doing, *individually,* to show kindness and love to people in need?

3. She performed *small* acts of kindness (v. 39). Dorcas made clothes for widows. That was her good work! It may not seem to be a monumental service, or something particularly noteworthy, but to the widows living in Joppa in the first half of the first century, it meant the world. Because of her small acts of kindness, Dorcas was deeply mourned after her death. Peter was called and restored her life, and as a result—many believed in the Lord (v. 42)! Dorcas, through her own simple display of compassion, had a significant impact on her community, and ultimately, a profound impact on the church.

4. She was *remembered* for her good works (v. 39). Imagine all of the widows, holding the precious clothes that she had made for them, with tears running down their faces as they stood beside the body of Dorcas in the upper room. They were brokenhearted! They must have been thinking about what a blessing she had been to them and all of the goodness she had shown them! The disciples in Joppa had received word that the apostle Peter was in the nearby city of Lydda. Everyone knew that he had the power to heal; maybe he could bring Dorcas back to them? Two men went to find Peter, and they begged him to come and help. Dorcas and her good works would not be forgotten!

5. She performed good works *"while she was with them"* (v. 39). Dorcas took advantage of opportunities to help others. This is what we are commanded to do in Scripture! Galatians 6:10 says, "Therefore, as we have opportunity, let us do good to all, especially to those who are of the household of faith." When she could, while she was with them, as the occasions presented themselves, Dorcas did good works. One day, each of us will leave this world. Looking back on our lives, how many opportunities will we see that we took to show kindness to someone? There will come a time when it will be too late. While we are here, we need to go about doing good, like Dorcas did, and like Jesus did.

IN HIS STEPS

Jesus fulfilled the words spoken by the prophet Isaiah, "He Himself took our infirmities and carried away our diseases" (Matthew 8:17, Isaiah 53:4). While Jesus walked on this earth, he healed the sick and had compassion for the lost. He showed love and mercy to sinners. He treated people with kindness and comforted the hurting. His entire life was lived in service to others.

Read the words describing Jesus in Acts 10:36-38,

"The word which God sent to the children of Israel, preaching peace through Jesus Christ—He is Lord of all—that word you know, which was proclaimed throughout all Judea, and began from Galilee after the baptism which John preached: how God anointed _____ of _____ with the Holy Spirit and with power, who went about _____ _____ and _____ all who were oppressed by the devil, for _____ was with Him."

OUR DAILY WALK

See every moment of every day as an occasion to do good works. In fact, see your whole life as a collection of good works offered to God. In Ephesians 2:10 we read, *"For we are His workmanship, created in Christ Jesus for good works, which God prepared beforehand that we should walk in them."* Everything that we do is by his grace and for his purpose—this is the heart of the Christian!—and our ultimate goal is that God will be glorified.

Ask yourself the questions: What am I doing? How am I helping? Then look for opportunities! Be good and do good…two very simple principles that can have an eternal impact. *Obey God and help people.* What if everyone lived by those rules? *Follow the Bible and treat others with kindness.* Simple, yes; but it could also be life-changing, or even better, *soul-saving.*

Give your time, your things, your self, your love, and share your life! You can do good works in so many different ways for so many different people. Pray for God to open up doors of opportunity for you to do good works. Ask for him to use you to do good in the lives of others. I believe he will open those doors, and he will use you. Give him the glory!

In Matthew 25:31-46, Jesus told a story about the judgment. He talked about how all nations will be gathered up and then separated into two groups: the sheep and the goats. The sheep will be set on the right hand of the King and the goats on the left; the sheep will inherit the kingdom, and the goats will be sent away into everlasting punishment. What distinguished one group from another? Good works! The sheep fed the hungry, clothed the naked, visited the sick, went to see those in prison, and gave shelter to strangers. And Jesus said, *"Assuredly, I say to you, inasmuch as you did it to one of the least of these My brethren, you did it to Me."*

The sheep are out doing good! They're changing the world for the better! They are showing kindness to people, and at the same time, they are showing kindness to Jesus.

We don't do good works for our own honor; we do them in the name of Jesus, so that people might come to know him and discover what it means to be his disciple. It's all about him.

At the end of the day, have you been a sheep or a goat?

STRENGTH

What should be your motivation for doing good works? (Ephesians 2:10-11)

What do you hope will be the result?

Although it should not be your motivation, how do you personally benefit from doing good for others?

TRIALS

What is your greatest barrier to doing good works? (Is it time? Determining a need? Not sure what you can do?)

If we aren't careful, we might think that good works might earn us blessings or rewards. What does Philippians 2:3-4 say? How can this be applied to good works?

Sometimes we might think of good works as grandiose expressions rather than small acts of kindness. Awe-inspiring deeds can be just that, but what can be the trouble in having that expectation all of the time?

ENCOURAGEMENT

What can you do? What would you like to be remembered for?

Think about the stories of the fish, the Frisbee, the flashback, the fingerprints, and the flowers. How can these inspire you when it comes to walking in good works? Next to each category below, write down some ideas of how you might use that gift to help someone else. Consider how you can use these gifts daily, or continually, to show kindness.

Your time –

Your possessions –

Your life –

Your self –

Your love –

PRAYER

I give glory to you, God, for the goodness you showed me in sending Jesus Christ to be my Redeemer. I praise you for his perfect life and willingness to go to the cross. I pray that I keep his sacrifice always in my thoughts as I go throughout my day and see people who need my help. I pray that as I remember what he did for me, I will do for others to bring glory to your name.

I want for my life to be a continual good work. I want to be full of kindness, like Dorcas. Help me uncover my own abilities to serve others and help me find opportunities to use them each day.

I pray that as your church, we will do good for your glory. I hope that we will do so much to change the lives of people for the better that the entire world will take notice. Open my eyes to the needs of the hurting and the lonely. Use my hands to make a difference.

In Jesus' Name, Amen

WALK WITH THE DOC

Walking tip: Walk to be an example

"Worry not that people listen to you; worry most that they watch you." – Heifetz. *"Do as I say, not as I do"* is perhaps the weakest of all admonitions. It is by our actions that we set the example. To understand the full benefits of walking and not walk would be folly. To know it and not share it would be selfish. Everyone can benefit from your example, but especially the young, who could potentially experience tremendous lifelong benefits as a result. As a walker, being an example is more than simply being seen; it also involves making an active effort to encourage others to get moving.

TAKE ACTION!

This week encourage someone else to begin a walking program. Talk to your friend about the activity you've been doing, or tell her about the walking plans in the back of this book. If you have noticed a change in the way you feel as a result of walking, share that with someone. You can make a difference in someone's life!

CHAPTER FOURTEEN

LEAVE YOUR PAST BEHIND
Walk in Newness of Life

"Therefore we are buried with Him through baptism into death, that just as Christ was raised from the dead by the glory of the Father, even so we also should walk in newness of life" (Romans 6:4).

I read something interesting the other day. A study, conducted by researchers at Georgetown University, found that butterflies remember aspects of their lives as caterpillars. This may sound completely unremarkable at first, but consider what takes place in the chrysalis. The caterpillar experiences a metamorphosis: *a complete change in form, structure, or function as a result of development.* I've heard it compared to recycling, in which something entirely new is created from something else. A large portion of the caterpillar's body is broken down to the stem cell level, and the stem cells then put themselves back together into a different shape, referred to as *holometabolism.* It is amazing that, through that process, the butterfly emerges and can even recall some of its previous life as a larva.

This should sound very familiar to the Christian! We can relate to the butterfly because of the complete life change that is experienced through baptism. Before being immersed into Christ (Galatians 3:27), we were wingless and...well, wormlike. Sin bound us to the world, left us belly crawling, growing larger and larger as we continually munched on the cares of the world. Then, God saved us! Through the free gift of grace, God provided an opportunity for transformation. All we have to do is listen to his directions that will lead us to a safe place, believe in his promise for our future, shed our old skins, declare Jesus Christ as his Son, and then enter into the watery chrysalis of baptism to become new creatures with new lives.

"Therefore, if anyone is in Christ, he is a new creation; old things have passed away; behold, all things have become new" (2 Corinthians 5:17).

"Therefore we were buried with Him through baptism into death, that just as Christ was raised from the dead by the glory of the Father even so we also should walk in newness of life" (Romans 6:4).

Now, here is where the Christian and the butterfly travel a different pathway. Inasmuch as butterflies exhibit behaviors that are reminiscent of their former lives as larvae, the Christian must *"not remember the former things nor consider the things of old"* (Isaiah 43:18). In his life, Paul recognized that he had not yet reached the ultimate prize of eternal glory, and then committed himself to forgetting the past and reaching forward to the future as he pressed toward that goal (Philippians 3:13-14).

For the Christian, it's not remembering how bad life was as a caterpillar—it's the daily reminder that we are butterflies because of Jesus and the sacrifice that he made for us on the cross. Every day we "transform" and remind ourselves that we are not of this world; we've left behind our lives as caterpillars, and we renew our minds. Not my words, but Paul's, as he wrote to the Romans about giving their lives over completely to God (Romans 12:2).

As butterflies, there should be an obvious difference in the way we look and behave from caterpillars. If we continue to read chapter 12, in Paul's letter to the Romans we find many suggestions he gave as to how Christians should conduct themselves—actions that would help distinguish between that *"eww-ww"* stage of life as a larva to the *"ahhhhhh"* stage of life as a majestic butterfly!

When I see a butterfly, I feel humbled by its beauty and the power that God has to make such an awesome change. I wonder if the butterfly remembers what it felt like to crawl as it gracefully takes flight? I am thankful that because I left my old life behind and accepted God's grace through obedience in baptism, I don't have to remember. I pray that I never take for granted the opportunity God has given me to fly above this world, and always remember that without him, I wouldn't have the wings to try.

New Creations

Christians, like butterflies, are new creations with new lives. We know that for the butterfly, a new life is characterized by wings and flight, but what does the new life of a Christian look like? It should look completely different from the life before baptism— before dying to the old man and rising up out of the water as a new man. It's a life that is characterized by a new way of living, but what *is* that new way?

In Ephesians 4:17-24, Paul wrote to the church about their lives as new creations in Christ and how that should affect the way they live. He encouraged them to forget the past and live new lives that are centered in Christ and characterized by continual renewal of the mind.

Leave the Past in the Past

The first thing Paul told the Christians was that, as new people, they should no longer walk like the Gentiles (v. 17). It's an urgent plea, made with authority! Paul says, "Stop!" The word "Gentile" in this context is not being used to describe ethnicity or a specific race of people, instead it's referring to those who are unconverted, or unsaved. Paul continues from there to describe the Gentile lifestyle that they should leave in the past because it is a lifestyle that is spiritually destitute.

First, he refers to their old walk as living "in the futility of their mind." The word *futile* is defined as "incapable of producing any useful result." In other words, their previous mindset was pointless. Paul did not mean that they weren't intelligent, but that their way of thinking was completely empty. Even though they were able to think, their understanding was darkened as well because they lived in a state of spiritual darkness (v. 18).

He goes on to say that in their old lives they were "alienated from the life of God, because of the ignorance that was in them, because of the blindness of their heart." Paul makes the point that this isolation from God was willful; they chose to ignore him! They knew the Truth, but chose to reject it! They were "past feeling," meaning they had become hard, like callouses on the skin that no longer feel pain. Their consciences had rejected the Truth for so long that it no longer mattered, and they became comfortable with sin.

As a result, Paul said that they "gave themselves over to lewdness; to work all uncleanness with greediness." Lewdness is defined as "immoral behavior which throws off all restraint and flaunts itself without regard to decency."

That immoral behavior is defined in verse 19 as "all uncleanness" and not only that, but that "uncleanness" was also pursued with greediness. Paul was speaking about their unquenchable desire for more and more and more impurity. This behavior was all around the Christians in Ephesus, in Rome (Romans 1:18-25), in Corinth (1 Corinthians 6:9-11), and it is all around us in the world today!

When I was in 7th grade, I did a science project on the filtration of salt water which reminds me of the old life of the Gentiles that Paul was describing. Their way of living was the spiritual equivalent of a person dying of thirst and then drinking salt water for relief. The same is still true today. Sin is deceptive. It looks satisfying and people think it will relieve their thirst, so they indulge in it more and more. In reality, they are dying of thirst right in front of you.

"But you did not learn Christ in this way" (v. 20, NASB).

This is the old life, and it's not life at all. It's a living death. Paul wanted his readers to know that if you have been made a new person in Christ, you must no longer live this way!

New People, New Life

As new people, we live new lives (vv. 20-24). Paul explained that new people have learned a different way of living that is centered in Christ. He said that they had heard Christ and been taught the truth by Him, and now these changes should be evidenced in their lives:

- Lay aside the old self (v. 22)
- Be renewed in the spirit of their minds (v. 23)
- Put on the new self (v. 24)

Laying aside the old self involves abandoning our former way of life, prior to our conversion, a life that is characterized by corruption and deceitful lust. The phrase "put off" indicates a completed action, meaning that it was something done at one point in time. Putting on the new self, which is characterized by true righteousness and holiness, is an act of God. He creates the new person! The phrase "put on" also indicates a completed action. Both the "putting off" and "putting on" occur at baptism, and the effects continue in the process of renewal which continually takes place in the mind of a Christian.

In verse 23, tucked in between the laying aside of the old and putting on the new is where we find the command to be renewed in the spirit of our mind. "Spirit of the mind" refers to our inner thought patterns, or the direction of our thinking. Unlike the "putting on and off," the verb form of "be renewed" does not indicate a completed act, but rather an on-going process. It's also in passive form, so it refers to something that is being done in us, not by us. The renewal of our minds is done by the Holy Spirit through the Word of God.

Here is a summary of the new life: Upon hearing the Gospel and responding to the Truth in faithful obedience, we surrender ourselves in baptism according to God's will. In that moment, in the watery grave, we put off our old self that is marked by sin and dying; and we put on our new self, created by God, that is marked by truth and righteousness. Each and every day we are renewing our minds as we reflect on where we've come from and where we are going. We renew our minds through the Word of God, which is the Truth. As we read and apply the Word to our lives, new values begin to replace old values; new ways of thinking replace the old ways; and the Spirit can be seen working in our lives as new creatures to give us comfort, guidance, strength, and hope.

A WALKING WARRIOR

In one of my favorite Andy Griffith episodes, Barney struggles to stay awake while listening to a visiting preacher present a lesson on the importance of slowing down. After the service, Barney meets the preacher and (clearly not having paid attention) says, "That's one subject you just can't talk enough about: *sin.*" As they walk away, Andy tells Barney, with a hint of exasperation, "He didn't talk about *sin!*"

In the Bible we find that the apostle Paul often spoke on the subject of sin. Within his letters to the early churches he defined sin, warned against sin, and offered his own confessions of sin. Memories of how he persecuted the church, before becoming a Christian, plagued his mind, and he had to remind himself to forget what was behind and continue pressing on toward the ultimate goal. His past haunted him.

To a mob in Jerusalem before being taken to the barracks Paul said, *"I perse-cuted this Way to the death, binding and delivering into prisons both men and women"* (Acts 22:4).

To King Agrippa, he said, *"Indeed, I myself thought I must do many things contrary to the name of Jesus of Nazareth. This I also did in Jerusalem and many of the saints I shut up in prison, having received authority from the chief priests; and when they were put to death, I cast my vote against them. And I punished them often in every synagogue and compelled them to blaspheme; and being exceedingly enraged against them, I persecuted them even to foreign cities"* (Acts 26:9-11).

Paul felt the suffocating guilt of sin. In his first letter to the church in Corinth, he wrote, *"For I am the least of the apostles, who am not worthy to be called an apostle, because I persecuted the church of God"* (1 Corinthians 15:9).

The Old Man and the New Man

Paul may have questioned his worth, but he also understood that he was forgiven of his past sins. He knew that he had put off the old man and put on the new man. In the book of Acts and throughout his letters you can see a distinct difference in the way he lived his old life in sin and in the way he lived his new life in Christ.

This man, who formerly consented to the death of Christians (Acts 8:1), also earnestly expected and hoped to magnify Christ, without shame, through his life or by his death (Philippians 1:20-21).

This man, who committed men and women to prisons for practicing Chris-tianity (Acts 8:3), also became an ambassador in chains for the Gospel (Ephesians 6:19-20).

This man, who tried to destroy God's church (Galatians 1:13), also told the saints in Rome that there is no condemnation to those who are in Christ Jesus for those who walk according to the Spirit (Romans 8:1).

This man, who had been deceived by sin (Romans 7:11), also approached the end of his life "having fought the good fight" and "having kept the faith" (2 Timothy 4:7).

This man, who considered himself to be "chief of sinners" (1 Timothy 1:15), also wrote about a crown of righteousness that would be given to him by the Lord on Judgment Day (2 Timothy 4:8).

Grace, Faith, and Forgiveness

How could Paul feel unworthy but have such confidence in his salvation? It's because Paul faithfully responded to God's exceedingly abundant grace which allowed him to walk in newness of life.

"And I thank Christ Jesus our Lord who has enabled me, because He counted me faithful, putting me into the ministry, although I was formerly a blasphemer, a persecutor, and an insolent man; but I obtained mercy because I did it ignorantly in unbelief. And the grace of our Lord was exceedingly abundant, with faith and love which are in Christ Jesus" (1 Timothy 1:12-14).

"Therefore, having been justified by faith, we have peace with God through our Lord Jesus Christ, through whom also we have access by faith into this grace in which we stand and rejoice in hope of the glory of God" (Romans 5:1-2).

In Acts 22, Paul recounted the story of his conversion before the Jewish mob. He described how he had been traveling the road to Damascus and had heard the voice of the Lord. He explained how the Lord had instructed him to go into the city where he would be told what he needed to do. He remembered how Ananias had come to him, restored his sight, and declared that he had been chosen by God to be His witness to all men. Ananias had said to him, "And now why are you waiting? Arise and be baptized, and wash away your sins, calling on the name of Lord." And Paul did.

Paul was not saved on the road to Damascus. He was saved when he became obedient to God's grace by washing away his sins through baptism. He believed in his forgiveness. He felt sure of his salvation. He never denied his sinful past, but he never let it hold him back from living a new life for Christ in the present. It was because of Paul's faithful response to God's exceedingly abundant grace that he, the chief of sinners, was able to become—and is forever remembered as being—a chief apostle.

IN HIS STEPS

The only reason we are able to live a new life is because of the death and resurrection of Jesus Christ. Our old man is crucified with him through baptism, and we rise up out of the water as a new man, no longer a slave to sin! Jesus lives! And because he lives, we have hope!

Romans 6:4 says, "Therefore we were _____ with Him through _____ into death, that just as Christ was _____ from the _____ by the glory of the Father, even so we should also walk in _____ of _____."

OUR DAILY WALK ————————————————————————

Christians are new creatures. They have been buried with Christ in baptism, and they have risen from that watery grave to walk in a new life. Living a new one requires leaving the old one. You can't be in the same place doing the same things you were doing before. You're changed. You're wearing new clothes, not old worn out garments.

One time our family was driving down to visit my husband's parents. Along the way, we passed the church building where they worshiped, and our daughter, Evie, looked out the window and yelled, "Hey, that's Paw Paw and Ro Ro's church!"

Beside the building is a cemetery and when Evie saw it she added, "…and there's where all their friends are!"

Whether their friends are there or not, you won't find Paw Paw and Ro Ro spending all of their time at the cemetery because they are continuing to enjoy life. In the same way, as Christians, we are living a new life in Christ, which means we're not hanging out among the spiritually dead. We're not lingering around tombstones and mausoleums. We've left our chrysalis grave and now we're new creatures. Alive! Flying to new places, filling ourselves with new food, and resting our hope on new things.

Walking in newness of life calls for regular closet checks. What garments do you have hanging up in your closet? Are they new, or do you still have the garments that were yours before you became a Christian? Those old clothes are stained with sin; our new clothes have been completely cleaned!

Are you washed in the blood,
In the soul cleansing blood of the Lamb?
Are your garments spotless?
Are they white as snow?
Are you washed in the blood of the Lamb?

Walking in newness of life also requires on-going self-evaluation. Ask yourself these questions as you walk through your day:

How have I changed since becoming a Christian? How am I continuing to change?
How am I renewing my mind today?
Am I letting influences of the world creep into my heart? My home?
Am I leaving the past in the past and pressing forward?
Have I thanked God for his gift of grace? *(Without it, we'd have no hope for newness of life!)*

Remember the evidence that was presented after Jesus had been resurrected from the dead: there was an empty tomb, discarded burial clothes, and people saw him alive again. Can this evidence be seen in your life?

An old life left behind after a watery burial!
Garments of sin thrown aside!
Eye-witness testimony to the new life you are living!

STRENGTH

> **When we are born again and begin walking a new life in Christ, why do we no longer have to fear death? Read these Scriptures: 1 Corinthians 15:55-57; 2 Corinthians 5:8; Philippians 1:21-23; Hebrews 2:14-15.**

Science tells us that physical life requires water, light, and nutrients. The same is true for spiritual life. How are each of those represented in the life of a Christian? (Find the Scriptures that tell us!)

How do your actions testify to the new life that can be found in Christ?

TRIALS

Sometimes we feel guilty when we think back on our former life, or when we find ourselves trying on those old comfortable sweaters of sin. What do we know about the blood of Jesus? (Ephesians 1:7; 1 John 1:7-9). What reassurance does this give you?

What is the greatest challenge to living a new life in Christ? How can it be overcome?

Do you have old sinful influences that continue to creep into your life? What can you do to keep those influences out?

ENCOURAGEMENT

When people in the world see us, do they yearn for the life we are living? As new men and women in Christ, walking in new lives, built on new hope, we are the most blessed! I challenge you to make a list of 100 blessings that are a part of your life. Not all of these have to be directly related to your spiritual life, although, if you are Christian, I'm sure many of them will be! Be very specific—this is going to be a *long* list!

Remind yourself of your blessings often. It's easy to take them for granted; especially the ones we enjoy daily!

One morning, as I was on my way to teach a women's class at the prison, I wrote the following poem entitled, "Wings." We were talking about new lives and new behaviors that day, and I thought the image of a butterfly would be helpful to use in describing the way we are changed when we become Christians. What a blessing it is that Jesus has given us wings to fly! It really touched the hearts of the ladies, so I thought I'd share it here, too:

Wings

I can still remember well the days before my wings,
Munching on the leaves of sin and other worldly things.

Crawling on my belly but in hope of something more;
Seeing birds above me and the lovely way they soar.

Then I heard a voice that said, "You, too, my friend, can fly—
Make the choice to make the change, and tell the worm 'goodbye'!"

I went beneath the water in a dark cocoon-like grave,
I left my past behind me—no more a sinful slave.

Now I'm flying high, and I'm a slave to better things;
I'm thankful Jesus changed me, made me new, and gave me wings!

by Lori Boyd

PRAYER

I praise you, Lord, for your power to take the old and make it new! I praise you for being the Giver of life and the Defeater of death! I praise you for changing me when I buried my sinful past in the waters of baptism! I praise you for your goodness and mercy!

Dear God, forgive me when I sin. Forgive me when I know the right thing to do, but fail to do it. Remove my guilt. Help me to resist temptations.

As I make the effort daily to renew my mind, help me to stay focused on your Word. Help me to find guidance in the Scriptures and help me grow in knowledge and understanding. I humbly ask for wisdom as I walk each day.

Thank you for your Son Jesus Christ! I am eternally grateful that he lives again!

In his name I pray, Amen

WALK WITH THE DOC
Walking tip: Walk for purification

Would you want to bathe in your old bath water? I am certain that your response would be a resounding "No!" But, why not? The short answer is because it's nasty. And yet, that is essentially what is happening if you are sedentary and not well-hydrated. God has provided a means for the body to rid itself of waste and toxins. The body does this in part by the lymphatic system. The cells (which are the units of function in the body) produce waste, which is carried away by the tissue fluid that bathes the cells. The fluid is transported by the lymphatic ducts and enters into the circulatory system where it is carried to the kidneys and liver to be detoxified and then excreted. Walking enhances lymphatic flow, and drinking lots of water leads to increased dilution, which is the solution to pollution. Remember, water and walks to detox!

TAKE ACTION!

For the next week, pay close attention to your daily water intake. To determine the amount of water you should drink every day, use this simple formula:

Body weight in pounds = the # of fluid ounces per day

(If you are involved in moderate or vigorous exercise, you may need to drink even more!)

Keep this in mind: "The solution to pollution is dilution!"

CHAPTER FIFTEEN
REMEMBER WHO YOU ARE
Walk Worthy

"For this reason we also, since the day we heard it, do not cease to pray for you, and to ask that you may be filled with the knowledge of His will in all wisdom and spiritual understanding; that you may walk worthy of the Lord, fully pleasing Him, being fruitful in every good work and increasing in the knowledge of God; strengthened with all might, according to His glorious power, for all patience and longsuffering with joy; giving thanks to the Father who has qualified us to be partakers of the inheritance of the saints in the light" (Colossians 1:9-12).

Remember who you are! If there were one rule, one piece of advice I could give my children to take with them on their individual walks to the Promised Land, it would be: *Remember who you are.* Keep 1 Peter 2:9 close to your heart, *"But you are a chosen generation, a royal priesthood, a holy nation, His own special people, that you may proclaim the praises of Him who called you out of darkness into His marvelous light."*

When you are struggling to forgive...remember who you are. When you feel like there is no hope...remember who you are. When it seems as though God has forgotten you...remember who you are. Walk daily in a way that is consistent with your identification in the Lord. You are a child of God... *live like it!*

Worthy of Friendship

In worship we sometimes sing the song, "Jesus is All the World to Me,"written by Will L. Thompson; it is a song about the friendship of Jesus. Each stanza describes facets of Jesus' character, which prove him to be the truest friend we will ever have—in this life and the life to come. We sing the lyrics *"I have found a friend in Jesus"* and *"There's not a friend like the lowly Jesus,"* words that beautifully illustrate the nature of Jesus. This idea of Jesus being our friend is comforting, powerful, and true!

Jesus is our friend because he knows us (Psalm 139:1-18).

Jesus is our friend because he loves us (John 13:34).

Jesus is our friend because he has revealed to us what he heard from his Father (John 15:15).

Jesus is our friend because he intercedes for us in Heaven (Romans 8:34).

Jesus is our friend because he died for us. In John 15:13, he told his disciples, *"Greater love has no one than this, than to lay down one's life for his friends."* In the ultimate display of friendship, Jesus sacrificed himself on the cross to pay for our sins so that he might bring us to God (1 Peter 3:18).

Through these and many other examples found in Scripture, I can confidently say, *"Jesus is my friend."* However, as that truth permeates my heart, it inevitably gives rise to a new thought; a question that requires honest self-evaluation: *"Am I a friend to him?"*

Considering that, my mind goes back to one day when I was standing in the kitchen and looking out the window above the sink. My son Briggs was jumping on the trampoline while executing a series of punches and kicks toward an unseen enemy. I could tell his lips were moving, and I imagine he was hurling intimidating threats and presenting attractive ultimatums. I walked outside to find out if the odds were looking to be in his favor as the battle raged on. *"Briggs! How's it going?"* I yelled. Breathless, and without a break in action, he answered, *"It's good! Me and Jesus and God are just taking on these guys!"*

At five years old, Briggs could not have had a full understanding of the awesome sovereignty of God, but he did know that with God and Jesus on his side, he would win! I love that he picked them as his teammates; I love that for him it felt completely natural to be fighting bad guys with them; and I love that he wanted to jump on the trampoline with God and Jesus as if they were his best friends.

As we grow and mature as Christians, we learn more about the nature of God through Bible study and gain a greater understanding of his power and his holiness. In Scripture we read *"The friendship of the Lord is for those who fear him."* When David wrote those words in Psalm 25:14, he used the Hebrew word *yare*, which is translated "fear," and in this context carries the meaning "to revere." If we want to be a friend of the Lord, we have to honor, respect, and worship him. We have to recognize him as the Almighty Creator of the world and kneel before him with a humble heart and a sincere desire to do his will.

In John 15:14, Jesus told his disciples that they were his friends if they did what he commanded. When we obey Jesus, we express our friendship and demonstrate our love for him (John 14:15). We cannot be his friend if we ignore his Word.

We are also being a friend to Jesus when we are kind to others. In Matthew 25, Jesus told a story about the righteous and unrighteous on the Day of Judgment. To those seated on His right hand, the King said, *"Come you blessed of My Father, inherit the kingdom prepared for you from the foundation of the world: for I was hungry and you gave Me food; I was thirsty and you gave Me drink; I was a stranger and you took Me in; I was naked and you clothed Me; I was sick and you visited Me; I was in prison and you came to Me...Assuredly, I say to you, inasmuch as you did it to one of the least of these My brethren, you did it to Me"* (vv. 34-36, 40). When we show friendship to others, we show friendship to Jesus.

What a privilege to be referred to as *"a friend of God"* like Abraham was in James 2:23! I want to live my life in such a way that I might wear the same title. When God looks down from Heaven, I pray he will find me, in all my faithful imperfection, worshiping him, obeying him, and serving him through kindness to others, so that he can say the words, *"She is my friend."*

Worthy of Fragrance

I love the smell of my husband's cologne. I love the smell of coffee brewing. I love the smell of a newborn baby. I love the smell of wood burning. I love the smell of the ocean.

On the other hand, there are smells that I definitely do not love. A couple of years ago when Pearl, our lab-shepherd mix, found herself on the receiving end of a skunk's warning, I discovered a new level of detest for that particular smell.

Fragrance is an experience. By that I mean, it affects you personally, whether in a good way or a bad way. When you smell something, you react to it, even if only on a subconscious level. Here is the condensed version of how it works:

The chemoreceptors in your nose are stimulated when they detect an odor. They send electrical impulses to the brain where the sensations are interpreted and converted to perception, which is recognition of the smell. What is really amazing is that the olfactory bulb, where all of this occurs in the brain, is a part of the limbic system—our emotional center. This system plays an important role in our mood and memory, and "smells" are processed in the very same place; which is why certain smells can stimulate feelings of happiness or sadness.

Another important fact about fragrance is that it is the byproduct of something else. It is usually our first indication of what is occurring in the world around us, and it is what lingers with us long after its source has been removed.

There is a wonderful scripture found in 2 Corinthians that reads, *"For we are a fragrance of Christ to God among those who are being saved and those who are perishing"* (2 Corinthians 2:15). When you consider the word "fragrance," this scripture takes on a beautiful meaning and a considerable charge. Christ came to this world, lived, died, and rose to live in Heaven again. While he is no longer physically among us, in the eyes of God, his fragrance remains earthbound, in the form of a Christian.

If, as Christians, we are the fragrance of Christ, what affect are we having on the world around us? What feelings do we stimulate in others? The aroma of Christ should be lovely. It should be comforting and sweet. It should be peaceful and approachable. Is this how we are perceived? To be the fragrance of Christ is an honor. Are we living worthy of that responsibility? Maybe we should start by asking, how would Christ *want* to be perceived, and then live in a way that would be pleasing to him.

Worthy of Fellowship

Not only do we have the privilege of enjoying friendship with the Lord and living as his fragrance on this earth, but we also have the honor of fellowship with him. 1 John 1:3 says, *"that which we have seen and heard we declare to you, that you may have fellowship with us; and truly our fellowship is with the Father and with His Son Jesus Christ."*

"Fellowship" is translated from the Greek word *koinonia* which is defined as "sharing in common, holding a mutual interest, mutual activity, a partnership with each other, participating together." How do we fellowship with God?

If you read a little further in 1 John, you'll find in verse 6 that in order to have fellowship with God, we can't be walking in darkness. He *is* the light, and if we want to fellowship with him, then we have to be walking in the light as well. That means living according to the Truth. *(Remember those cave crickets?).*

Fellowship with God happens when we read, study, and meditate on his Word. It happens when we approach his throne in prayer. It happens when we worship him in spirit and in Truth. Then, our fellowship with God in the light will bring us into fellowship with other Christians!

The word *koinonia* is translated in different ways in different places in Scripture. For example, in Acts 2:42, *koinonia* is translated "fellowship;" in Romans 15:26 it's translated "contribution;" also "communion" or "sharing" in 1 Corinthians 10:16; and "communicate" in Galatians 6:6. Each of these represent a way that Christians participate together or share a common interest.

Here are some ways that Christians fellowship with one another:

- In worship (1 Corinthians 10:16-17; Hebrews 10:23-25)
- In working for the Lord (Matthew 20:1)
- In faith (1 Corinthians 1:10; Philippians 1:27)
- In caring, bearing, sharing (1 Corinthians 12:26, Galatians 6:2, Romans 12:15)
- In salvation (Jude 3)
- In association with each other (Malachi 3:16)

There is harmony and unity among God's people because we have the common goal of walking in the light. That's where we'll find God, and when we walk there, we not only have fellowship with him, but with other Christians, too. This is a precious gift that comes with being a child of God—a gift that results in the encouragement and edification of brothers and sisters in Christ.

A WALKING WARRIOR

A loving father. An obedient son. A chosen people. A promise of inheritance. A hill to climb. A wooden load. A required sacrifice.

Two stories separated by two thousand years, and both a part of God's eternal purpose.

One ended in the salvation of the son.

The other ended in the salvation of the world.

"While God spared Isaac, the son of Abraham, He could not spare His own Son, Jesus, in order for His promise of blessing to be fulfilled" (Romans 8:32).

Faithful Abraham: a man called by God to leave the comforts of his home and move to a land he had never seen, with no idea how to get there, upon the promise for a family that he didn't have. And by faith, he obeyed. Abraham trusted God throughout all of his life. He based that trust on hope; the hope of a heavenly country. He lived a life of faith, and he died in faith. Hebrews 11:16 says, *"Therefore God is not ashamed to be called their God, for He has prepared a city for them."*

Abraham walked worthy and was assured of promises to come—eternal promises through Jesus Christ.

The Test

The greatest trial faced by Abraham required deeply grounded, unshakeable faith. He received the command to offer his only son, Isaac, as a sacrifice to God. It's as if every test he had encountered before was in preparation for this monumental moment. God had a plan to redeem mankind in order to achieve his eternal purpose, and that redemption would require a sacrifice.

God knew that it would take the death of his Son, Jesus, to reconcile man to him. Would his servant Abraham, the man from whom Jesus would descend, be willing to give his own begotten son to God? I can almost hear the questions: *Are you worthy Abraham? Would you do for Me, what I plan to accomplish through you?* It was the ultimate test. We find the story in Genesis 22.

God instructed Abraham saying, *"Take now your son, your only son Isaac, who you love, and go to the land of Moriah, and offer him there as a burnt offering on one of the mountains of which I shall tell you"* (Genesis 22:2).

The Results

When confronted with this unimaginable task, Abraham responded in faithful obedience.

FAITH— Paul wrote this powerful description of Abraham's faith in the book of Romans: *"He did not waver at the promise of God through unbelief, but was strengthened in faith, giving glory to God, and being fully convinced that what he had promised He was also able to perform. And therefore 'it was accounted to him for righteousness'"* (Romans 5:20-22). Abraham believed that God would provide. In Hebrews 10:17-19, we find that he had come to the conclusion that God would be able to raise Isaac from the dead following the offering.

Abraham never doubted that God would keep his promise. He wasn't sure how and he may not have understood the test at the time, but he placed his full trust in God.

OBEDIENCE— Abraham obeyed, went, dwelt, waited, and offered. These are words in Hebrews 11 that describe the way Abraham responded because of his faith. His faith was made perfect by his works (James 2:22). He believed and his belief resulted in action! God gave Abraham a test that required him to *do* something. God was looking for obedience, not just words and not just a good feeling in Abraham's heart; God wanted to see if Abraham would do what He had commanded him to do.

"By faith Abraham, when he was tested, offered up Isaac, and he who had received the promises offered up his only begotten son, of whom it was said, 'In

Isaac your seed shall be called"' (Hebrews 11:17). I cannot imagine that three-day walk up the mountain. I cannot imagine the building of the altar, the bounding of his child, the fielding of innocent questions, the stretching of his knife-wielding hand over the body of his son. I simply cannot imagine.

I praise God for Abraham's faith and obedience. I am eternally grateful. Abraham received a blessing that contained a promise—a promise of which you and I are heirs.

The Legacy

Abraham believed that God would keep His promises, and he demonstrated a willingness to obey regardless of the cost. As a result, Abraham was blessed.

"By Myself I have sworn, says the Lord, because you have done this thing, and have not withheld your son, your only son—blessing I will bless you, and multiplying I will multiply your descendants as the stars of the heaven and as the sand which is on the seashore; and your descendants shall possess the gate of their enemies. In your seed all the nations of the earth shall be blessed, because you have obeyed My voice" (Genesis 22:16-18).

Abraham's legacy is his faithful obedience that resulted in the blessing of all the nations of the earth through Jesus Christ. He was a walking warrior—worthy of the greatest promise ever made.

IN HIS STEPS

The angels cry out in Heaven with a loud voice saying,

"_____ is the _____ who was slain to re-

ceive _____ and _____ and wisdom, and

_____ and honor and glory and _____!"

(Revelation 5:13).

We walk worthy, because Jesus IS worthy!

How do we walk worthy of the Lord in our day to day lives? The theme verse for this chapter, Colossians 1:9-12, gives us specific instructions on what we can do to walk in a way that will be pleasing to God. Take a few seconds to read the text one more time.

The first thing we are told is to never stop praying. Paul wrote specifically that we should ask to be filled with the knowledge of God's will in all wisdom and understanding. As we fill ourselves up with those things, we will begin to walk in a way that is worthy of the Lord. We need to get in the habit of making prayer our initial response to everything!

I remember a couple of years ago at Bible Camp that it was late, and everyone was getting ready for bed. My daughter, Kate, came and found me, looking very worried. One of the girls in her cabin was homesick and wanted to leave. In fact, the counselors had already called her family to come pick her up. The little girl was sad because part of her wanted to stay, but the other part really wanted to go back home. My Kate's heart was breaking for her friend as she watched her pack her bag with tears falling down her cheeks. Kate said, "Mom, I really want to help. I've talked to her, and I've prayed with her, and I just don't know what else to do." I hugged that sweet girl of mine and said, "You've already done the very best thing you can do for her." Prayer should be the first thing that comes to our mind when we're looking for answers.

The second thing we are told is to be fruitful in every good work. Remember the F's (from chapter 13)! Be good and do good! To be fruitful means to be "abundantly productive." When we walk worthy of the Lord, we do every good work in such a way that the results will be rewarding.

Third, we should grow in our knowledge of God. This requires regular Bible study. We come to know God through his Word. The more we read and meditate on it, the more we understand his love, his goodness, his forgiveness, his judgments, his commands, his mercy, and his grace. It's difficult to try to walk worthy of something when you don't fully understand its worth. We discover the worth of the Lord through reading the story of his great love and redemption of man. He is most worthy.

Next we allow ourselves to be strengthened by God's power. We receive strength from God through his Word (Psalm 119:28) and through prayer (Psalm 22:19). He strengthens those who hope in him (Isaiah 40:31), who rejoice in him (Nehemiah 8:10), and who have given their hearts completely to him (2 Chronicles 16:9). Those who walk worthy of the Lord are strong.

And finally, we are to give thanks. Having a spirit of thanksgiving for God's mercy and grace and for all the spiritual blessings he has given us will help us to walk worthy. We should always be mindful of the sacrifice that was made so that our sins could be taken away. People who walk worthy of the Lord have a sincerely grateful heart.

STRENGTH

Remember what God has done for you! Continue reading in our text from Colossians 1:12 through verse 14. What does Paul, by inspiration, say that God has done for us?

What does he specifically say that we receive in Christ?

How should this influence the way that we walk?

TRIALS

We are surrounded by things in this world that want to keep us from walking worthy of the Lord. Temptations, distractions, suffering, persecution, and death—all of these will try our faith and can lead to a way of living that is either pleasing or unpleasing to the Lord.

How do we walk worthy in the face of wilderness trials?

I've mentioned a few times throughout this book that we have to remember that we are not perfect people. I think sometimes we feel like we have to be. We need to let go of that unrealistic and unhealthy perception! The devil uses guilt and resentment to weaken people in the church; he also uses hypocrisy and unrighteous judgment to keep people out. Walking worthy of the Lord does not mean walking perfectly. If that were the case, it would be an impossible and unfair expectation, and we would all be doomed to fail! That is not the intent of the God that we serve. God wants your love, your praise, and your faithful obedience. Remind yourself of the words written by David in Psalm 56:9, *"This I know: God is for me!"*

How do we walk worthy when we are sinners?

ENCOURAGEMENT

It can be difficult to express our gratitude to Almighty God. He, who has blessed us beyond measure, deserves our most humble thanksgiving; but sometimes I feel like I can't seem to communicate my love and appreciation enough. If you've ever felt that way, here is something for you to try:

Write God a "thank you" letter. Find a blank card, stationary, or just a piece of notebook paper and put your thoughts into written words. Think about what you are most thankful for, and tell God how you feel about it. You can reflect on our theme verse for this chapter (Colossians 1:9-12) and specifically the phrase, *"giving thanks to the Father who has qualified us to be partakers of the inheritance of the saints in the light."*

I can hear the voice of my mom teaching me how to write a nice "thank you" note: start with your greeting, express your appreciation for what you were given, mention how you are using or plan to use the gift, talk about what it means to you, express your appreciation again for the thoughtfulness you were shown, add a personal message, and then close your letter. (I am thankful for a mother who taught me and my sisters the value of note writing!) You can follow this same pattern in your letter for this exercise if it would be helpful.

Writing down your prayers or drawing a picture of how you are feeling can help you convey what's on your heart. If it ever seems that you can't find the words you want to say, try grabbing a pen and paper and see if you can write, or draw, your way over the hurdle. These would be beautiful to share with each other if you are in a class setting. How encouraging to hear letters of thanks written to our Heavenly Father!

PRAYER

Dear God and Father in Heaven, I know that I am not worthy of your grace and mercy. I know that the only reason I can humbly come before your presence is because your Son IS worthy and his cleansing blood washes away my sins.

I thank you for the living hope we have through the resurrection of Jesus Christ, and I thank you for the inheritance you have reserved for me in Heaven. I pray that you will help me to bear fruit in good works, to grow in knowledge, and to be strengthened by your power.

I pray that I live in a way that is pleasing to you. I want to be your friend, I want to be the fragrance of Christ, and I want to enjoy the benefits of fellowship with you as your child.

When trials come, keep me by your power through faith.

In Jesus' Name, Amen

WALK WITH THE DOC
Walking tip: Walk in the Wilderness

Maintaining one's strength is key to maintaining independence in the later years. It is weakness that leads to limitations in carrying out activities of daily living. As we age, there is the tendency to lose lean mass (muscle and bone) and become weaker. Walking combined with resistance training for upper body is a great way to maintain muscle tone and preserve bone strength. Nordic Walking, which utilizes poles, is a great form of exercise that very conveniently works the upper and lower body at the same time. Bear in mind the 'use it or lose it' expression. Deconditioning occurs rapidly. Avoid prolong periods of inactivity. Working out at least 3-4 times a week is imperative.

TAKE ACTION!

This week, combine your walking with some type of upper body resistance. Focus on the muscles in your neck and shoulders, arms, chest, back, and abdominals. Use hand held weights, walking poles, or simply pump your arms in rhythm with your steps. Also, be mindful of your abdominal muscles as you walk and keep them engaged.

CHAPTER SIXTEEN
WALK WITH THE FATHER
Walk with God

"So all the days of Enoch were three hundred and sixty-five years. And Enoch walked with God; and he was not, for God took him" (Genesis 5:23-24).

The first time she went, in the early hours of the morning, darkness still hung over the garden, and she wasn't alone. There were other women, and they had also seen: *The stone—rolled to the side, and the tomb—empty.* In fear, amazement, and joy, they ran to tell His disciples.

Later, she returned. After Peter and John came and saw and believed, Mary Magdalene went back. She stood alone outside the tomb crying—weeping over her dear friend. When she turned around, she saw a man standing there. "Why are you crying," He asked. "Who are you looking for?" She didn't recognize the man as being Jesus and assumed he was the gardener. Mary pleaded, "Sir, if you've carried Him somewhere else, tell me where you've laid Him and I will come and take Him away."

Then, He called out her name, "Mary!" And she knew. This was Jesus, her Healer, her Teacher, her Friend, and now her Savior. "Rabboni!" She answered. There, in the garden, they walked and talked together—Mary and her risen Lord (John 20:1-18).

In 1912, C. Austin Miles envisioned this scene as he penned the lyrics to the hymn, *In the Garden,* from the eyes of Mary Magdalene:

I come to the Garden alone, while the dew is still on the roses and the voice I hear falling on my ear, the Son of God discloses.

And He walks with me and He talks with me and He tells me I am His own,
and the joy we share as we tarry there, none other has ever known.

He speaks and the sound of His voice is so sweet the birds hush their singing
and the melody that He gave to me, within my heart is ringing.

She had walked with Jesus before. She had walked with him all throughout his ministry. But this walk was different. This time she walked with a deeper understanding. This time she not only walked with him as her friend, but also as her resurrected Lord. What did she say to him? What did he tell her? I can imagine the questions that she might have had, the direction she might have desperately sought, the fears she probably confessed.

What an honor for Mary to have been visited by Jesus outside of his tomb. What an incredible blessing to hear him speak her name in that moment, in that glorified form. What a gift to spend those moments in quiet communion, just Mary and her Redeemer, there in the garden, walking side by side.

Do you want to have a walking relationship with God? It's possible, and he is longing to walk with you.

Your Partner

God is your perfect walking partner. If you are walking with him, then you are undoubtedly walking in the right direction. Keeping your steps in line with his assures that you will reach the Promised Land. God possesses the characteristics of a walking partner whose very presence next to you on your journey is an invaluable blessing. This is what we learn about the nature of our God from Scripture:

*   He is wise (Romans 11:33).
*   He is faithful (1 Corinthians 1:9).
*   He is holy (Leviticus 19:2).
*   He is love (1 John 4:8).
*   He is just (Deuteronomy 32:4).
*   He is merciful (Ephesians 2:4-5).
*   He is good (Psalm 119:68).
*   He is gracious (Psalm 148:8).
*   He is forgiving (1 John 1:9).

We want…we *need*…him to be our walking partner. We *need* his attributes in our presence as we daily fight off influences in this world that are in direct opposition to his goodness and love. He can give us protection, and he can support us in our trials. In Jude 24-25 we read, *"Now to Him who is able to keep you from stumbling, and to present you faultless before the presence of His glory with exceeding joy, to God our Savior, who alone is wise, be glory and majesty, dominion and power, both now and forever. Amen."* That is incredibly comforting to me.

God is the perfect partner because he is always there, and he will never leave. Not only that, he has also told us that if we come close to him, he will come close to us. He is a reliable, ever-present, always available Friend. When you walk with God, his strength becomes your strength, his love becomes your love, and his peace becomes your peace. It is a walk of progression, enrichment, and reflection. The more time you spend walking with your Heavenly Father, the more you will hunger that time together.

The Price

You can't walk with God and with the world. That's the cost of the walk. It's not possible to partially walk with him. It's all or nothing. That doesn't mean that we have to be perfect in order for God to walk with us, but it does mean that we have a heart that is set on spiritual things and not on fleshly things. We have to walk in the light, where he dwells, and stay away from darkness where the desires of the world have found a comfortable place to hide.

In Amos 3:3, we read the question, *"Can two walk together unless they are agreed?"* To walk with God, our will and his must be in harmony. We can't have part of our spirit meet with God in communion while the other part shares an affection with the world. The two aren't compatible. They don't go together. Like the song we sing in worship: *Have thine affections been nailed to the cross? Is thy heart right with God? Does thou count all things for Jesus but loss? Is thy heart right with God?* In the book of James, the Bible says whoever wants to be a friend of the world makes himself an enemy of God (James 4:4). We have to choose our walking partner: Will it be the world, or will it be God?

Walking with God involves walking a road that is narrow. It includes letting go of evil companions, vain thoughts, improper conversations, and no longer living for sin. It might result in some form of persecution, or conflict with the world, or maybe even a lost relationship, but the more precious time we spend with our Creator, the more willing and capable we are of paying the price for the eternal blessings that will come from our walking together.

The Pleasure

It is a privilege and a gift to have the opportunity to walk with God. In the beginning, he created man and woman so that he could enjoy a walking relationship with them. We see him "walking in the garden in the cool of the day," in Genesis 3:8. They were his children, and he was their Father; together they were a family sharing a home, conversation, and company. And then the devil visited the garden, caused man to fall, and God's grace has been calling us Home ever since. One day, we'll be with him again, in spiritual form, in a spiritual place, and we'll be able to walk with him and talk with him. He will sing over us, and we will worship him!

In this life, we still have the ability to walk with God, and when we do, we experience a beautiful prequel to the life that is to come once we reach the Promised Land. We come to walk with God, here and now, through prayer and deep meditation on his Word. We walk with him when we choose to walk by the spirit and in the light. When we walk with him in these ways and draw our spirits close to him, then his nature becomes reflected in everything we say, and do, and even think because we spend so much time with him. Like Moses' face shone with the glory of God after being in his presence, so our lives will shine with God's glory when we walk with him. People will look at you and say, "I can tell she's been with God again."

Another reward that comes from walking with God is the growing love you will experience for him and the love that he will continue to pour over you. A walking relationship with God fosters a friendship that becomes stronger and stronger with time. You will come to better understand his love, grace, and mercy, and then discover a greater appreciation for what he has done for you and planned for you since before creation.

Walking with God prepares you for the final step that you will take from the wilderness into the Land of Promise. If he has been by your side through the desert, across the sand, and over the mountains, he will be with you in your final moments on earth as you enter into Heaven. He will hold your hand and walk with you right into eternity. And it won't be scary, and you won't be nervous, because he will be with you, walking beside you, just like always. Then be ready, because what happens next is so indescribable, so inconceivable, so beyond extraordinary, that our physical minds cannot form the thoughts to imagine it: *our first walk in Heaven with God.*

A WALKING WARRIOR

What an honor to be remembered as someone who walked with God and to have the timeless distinction of being a person who was pleasing to him. That's the legacy of Enoch, who the Bible tells us "did not see death" (Hebrews 11:5). Enoch is referred to four times in Scripture, and when we put together those snapshots of his life, it's easy to see why he is memorialized in the 11th chapter of Hebrews as being one of the great heroes of faith.

1. **GENESIS 5:19-24**—This is where we first read about Enoch. He's listed in the genealogy of Adam as a seventh generation descendant. We find that he was the son of Jared and fathered Methusaleh at the age of sixty-five. Then it says that after Methusaleh was born, Enoch *"walked with God three hundred years."* He is the first in Scripture to be given this life-style description, and later his great-grandson, Noah, would be described in the same way (Genesis 6:9). We also learn in this text that after 365 years of life, Enoch simply *"was not, for God took him."*

2. **LUKE 3:37**—In this verse, Enoch's name is listed in the genealogy of Jesus Christ through his earthly father, Joseph. The man who walked with God was in the family line of the Messiah.

3. **HEBREWS 11:5-6**—Here we learn more about the character of Enoch. He did not see death because God took him up to Heaven. It's almost as if after 300 years, God said "You've walked with me for so long and now I'm bringing you home, Enoch!" In verse 5, we're told that the reason God took Enoch was because he pleased Him. What does someone have to do in order to be pleasing to God? The very next verse gives us the answer: *"But without faith it is impossible to please Him, for he who comes to God must believe that He is, and that He is a rewarder of those who diligently seek Him"* (v.6). Enoch had faith, his faith made God happy, and he was rewarded

with a walk that took him straight from this world into the next!

4. **JUDE 14-15**—Finally, in the short epistle of Jude, Enoch is mentioned for the last time. In this text, we're also given a glimpse into his character, and we find a bold prophet who spoke out against evil and warned people about the judgment of the ungodly. (The word "ungodly" is used four times in these two verses!) He was a faithful preacher who spread a message that was definitely not popular at the time. Enoch lived in the pre-flood era, and the people around him were turning their backs on God. They weren't just indifferent to God; they were completely against him! However, in that environment, with those people surrounding him, Enoch's relationship with God grew closer and closer.

An Everlasting Walk

When it comes to our journey through life, our ambition should be to live in such a way that God would want to walk by our side. Enoch desired to have that type of relationship with his Creator, and they enjoyed 300 years of walking together on this earth. Enoch must have been a special man. We know that he was faithful. We know that he had harsh words for the wicked people of his time, and we also know that he believed in God and intensely wanted to be with him.

I wonder what Enoch did to develop that "walking" relationship with God? He wasn't perfect, because Ecclesiastes 7:20 says, *"For there is not a just man on earth who does good and does not sin"* and Romans 3:23 that tells us, *"All have sinned and fall short of the glory of God."* This fills me with hope! God walked with Enoch, but Enoch was not sinless. The fact that I am a sinner doesn't disqualify me as one of God's walking partners! So, if it wasn't that Enoch was perfect, what was it?

Enoch longed for God's company. He wanted to be with God. He hungered for that closeness. The way we find that in our lives today is through prayer, Bible study, prayer, worship, prayer, meditation, prayer, Christian fellowship, and prayer. I believe with all of my heart that a life of prayer is absolutely necessary to develop a walking relationship with God. When you talk to him, you have drawn yourself into his presence. He is right there with you in those times of prayer. When you worship, he is there. In fellowship, he is there. During Bible study, he is there speaking his words to you through Scripture.

I think Enoch looked for ways to connect with God personally and then made it a priority. Enoch had a wife and children, and as a prophet, he also worked for God, spreading His message throughout the lost world. Enoch was a busy man, but not too busy to walk with God! When I look at my day planner with all of its notes and scribbles and reminders; I need to remember Enoch. He didn't work God into his life; his life completely worked around God. What a lesson for you and me today.

This is what I like to think happened after 300 years of walking with his friend, Enoch, on this earth: God wanted to be with him in all of His fullness and glory. No one has seen God in that way except for Jesus (John 1:18). We don't have the ability, physically, to be in his presence (Exodus 33:20). He has revealed himself in other ways throughout time, but never in a complete sense. Enoch had been so faithful and his desire for a relationship was so great, that God simply didn't want to withhold himself any longer. God took his friend to Heaven, and I can only imagine, as Enoch stepped into the spiritual world and God welcomed him Home, how marvelous their new walk together must have been!

IN HIS STEPS

Sin separated us from God, but he brings us back to himself through his Son. We have the ability to walk with God only because of the soul cleansing blood of Jesus Christ. Read 1 Peter 3:18 and fill in the blanks:

"For _____ also suffered once for _____, the _____ for the _____ that He might bring us to _____, being put to _____ in the flesh but made _____ by the Spirit."

OUR DAILY WALK ─────────────────────────────

It should be our goal, every day, to walk in unbroken fellowship with our Heavenly Father. He longs for our company. I imagine him waiting for me, at the gate of a garden, because I told him that I wanted to spend more time with him. In my mind, he's sitting on a bench enjoying the sounds of nature and the beauty of his creation, but mindful that I'm not there. In the meantime, I'm very busy with my life, rushing through my day, working, taking care of my "to-do" list, and having a little fun mixed in there too, but somewhere deep down in my heart I know that God is waiting for me. I think to myself: *As soon as I finish everything, I'll meet up with him and at least we'll have a few minutes together. I can quickly tell him what I need, he can tell me what he expects from me, and then we can maybe schedule something for tomorrow.*

How incredibly sad! God wants so much more. He wants to walk with us all day long. He doesn't want a block of our time on one day of the week. He's not looking to be written in a fifteen-minute time slot on our day planners. We are his family and God wants an on-going relationship his children.

As we journey through this life and as we look toward our Promised Land, if God is our walking partner, we will experience a little of what Heaven holds while we're in the wilderness. If I'm walking with him I can know that I'm on the right course and that I'm headed in the right direction. By its very definition "walking" involves forward motion or advancement. When we walk with God, we are moving forward, or progressing, in our spiritual lives. There are a few practical ways we can know that we're walking with God daily.

First, we have to campout in the Scriptures. Don't just run through them. Open up your Bible and pitch your tent there. Spend quality time with the nature of God. Breathe him in deeply. Lie down in his tender mercy, close your eyes and feel the warmth of his enduring love, and reflect on the eternal significance of his grace. Allow the Spirit to fill you up with the beautiful, refreshing Truth.

Then, pray. This brings and keeps you together with God. You cannot have a relationship with someone you never talk to, especially when they long to hear your voice. Also, spend time in quiet meditation. Clear your mind of worldly things. Just let go of the busy, if only for a few minutes, and let the peace that comes from God permeate your mind.

Obey God, recognize his providence, and surround yourself with people who do the same.

232

Daily walking with God is a choice. It's the way that you decide you want to live your life. There is no better way, and there is no better company. He's waiting for you right now at the garden gate.

STRENGTH

What does it mean to walk with God?

What blessings come from having God as your walking partner?

What must you have in order to be pleasing to God? (Think specifically about Hebrews 11:6) How do you obtain it?

TRIALS

Walking with God involves sacrifice. What do you have to give up in order to walk with him?

How does the world make it difficult at times for you to walk with God?

ENCOURAGEMENT

We don't deserve to walk with him, but he loves us and his grace pulls us to him. God wants to walk with us! God longs for *you* to be his walking companion.

How would others describe your walk with God? How would Jesus describe it?

Write down what you imagine a physical walk with God would look like. How would it feel? Where would you go? What would you talk about?

PRAYER

Father, please walk with me. I crave your presence in my life. I so desperately want you to be with me as I walk through the wilderness and as I journey through each and every day of this life I am living on earth.

I long to close my eyes and hear the sound of your footsteps and to hear you gently call my name. One day, I know that we will walk together as friends, side-by-side and hand-in-hand. For now, while I am sojourning on this earth, I will search for you in your Word, I will reach out for you in prayer, I will look for you in the beauty of your creation, and I know you will be there. I will take every opportunity to draw near to you, and I believe that as you promised, you will draw near to me.

Thank you for your mercy and your grace. Thank you for Heaven and for showing me the way. Help me on my journey through the wilderness. May every step find me stronger in faith and closer to Home. When it is my time to enter, dear God, bring me safely into the Land you have promised and greet me with the comfort of your embrace.

I love you eternally.
In Jesus' Name, Amen

WALK WITH THE DOC

Walking tip: Walk with Focus

Life seems to be filled with constant distraction. Living in what appears to be a discordant world, we yearn for harmony. Too much to do, so little time. Our minds are brimming with thoughts and ideas with no prospect of order. Focus is the ability to dedicate one's attention to a main purpose or interest. Since it is impossible to do everything, one must live within that constraint and make choices, develop plans, establish milestones, set goals and allocate time. In that process, always keep in mind your priorities. Once you have created a manageable framework for your life, carry it out. Always have a built in measure of flexibility. Too much rigidity creates tension. We can examine this idea with the example of a walking program: When you're walking, you're walking, and that's it! Clear your mind and channel your attention, as desired, for the allotted time. When done, move on. This type of compartmentalization seems a bit OCD, but it isn't. Mastery of the mind creates tranquility. Take inventory of your life's goals often. Stay on track. Make the journey your destination.

As this study comes to a close, continue to find ways to walk! Stay committed to a walking program. Keep setting goals when it comes to your physical health and make time in your daily schedule to in order to accomplish them. Be a good steward of *all* that God has given you—mind, body, and spirit. Work to become stronger in each of those areas; the challenges and the trials that you encounter along the way will be worth the reward!

Most importantly, be purposeful in your daily walk as a Christian. Take steps that will make you stronger and will bring you closer to your spiritual Promised Land. The wilderness is rough sometimes, no question about it, but God has given us instructions on how to walk and where to walk so that we'll reach our destination. If we walk according to his will, we can know that we are walking Home.

Stay faithful, traveler! I hope to see you along the way!

WALKING PLANS
Just Keep Walking

WALKING DISTANCES *in Bible Times**

*Keep in mind that these Bible distances are based on estimations and vary slightly depending on the source

MILEAGE	DISTANCE	SCRIPTURE REFERENCE
0.5 Miles	One time around Jericho	Joshua 6 – The Israelites marched around the city of Jericho once a day for six days.
3.5 miles	Seven times around Jericho	Joshua 6 – On the seventh day, the Israelites marched around the city of Jericho seven times.
0.6 miles	Mount of Olives to Jerusalem (A Sabbath Day's journey)	Acts 1:9-12 – After witnessing Jesus' ascension into heaven from the Mount of Olives, his disciples returned to Jerusalem.
1 mile	Bethpage to Jerusalem	Matthew 21:1-11 – This tells of Jesus' triumphant entry into Jerusalem.

2 miles	Jerusalem to Bethany	Matthew 21:10-22 – Bethany was the home of Mary, Martha, and Lazarus. Jesus stayed with them after he drove the money changers out of the temple in Jerusalem (and on many other occasions as well).
6 miles	Bethlehem to Jerusalem	Luke 2:22 – Shortly after his birth, Jesus was taken to Jerusalem to be presented to the Lord.
7 miles	Jerusalem to Emmaus	Luke 24:13-27 – Jesus appeared to two of his disciples following his resurrection as they walked to the city of Emmaus.
11 miles	Across the Red Sea	Exodus 14 – This is the account of the Israelites crossing the Red Sea as they were pursued by the Egyptian army.
15 miles	Jerusalem to Jericho (The Jericho Road)	Luke 10:30 – This is the road that was traveled in the story of the good Samaritan.
15 miles	Bethlehem to the Valley of Elah	1 Samuel 17 – David tended his sheep in Bethlehem and delivered food to his brothers in the Valley of Elah where they were facing the Philistines in battle.
20 miles	Nazareth to Capernaum	Matthew 4:12 – Jesus traveled to Galilee where he would begin his ministry and call his first disciples.
20 miles	Shunem to Mount Carmel	2 Kings 4 – This is part of the route routinely traveled by Elisha as he prophesied to the Kingdom of Israel.

20 miles	Gaza to Hebron	Judges 16:3 – Samson carried the doors of the city gate and the gateposts from Gaza to Hebron after foiling a plot to end his life.
22 miles	Capernaum to Nain	Luke 7:1-17 – Jesus traveled from Capernaum (where he healed the centurion's servant) to Nain (where he raised a widow's only son from the dead).
25 miles	A day's journey	1 Kings 19:1-4 – Elijah went "a day's journey" into the wilderness after receiving a death threat from Jezebel.
30 miles	Jerusalem to Sychar (Jacob's Well)	John 4 – Jesus came to Sychar from Jerusalem and met a woman from Samaria as he sat by the well.
40 miles	Joppa to Caesarea	Acts 10 – Peter was in Joppa when he saw the vision of the unclean animals and left from there to preach the Gospel to Cornelius.
50 miles	Nazareth to the Jordan River	Mark 1:9 – Jesus walked to the Jordan to be baptized by John.
50 miles	Jerusalem to Gaza	Acts 8:26 – This is the desert road Philip was traveling when he encountered the Ethiopian eunuch.
57 miles	Caesarea to Jerusalem	Acts 11:1-18 – Peter returned to Jerusalem after converting Cornelius and his household.

63 miles *(divided 50 + 13)*	Hebron to Shechem (50 miles) Shechem to Dothan (13 miles)	Genesis 37:12-18 – Joseph was sent by his father to check on his brothers as they tended their flocks. He first went to Shechem only to find out that they had moved to the city of Dothan.
68 miles *(divided 42 + 26)*	Jerusalem to Antipatris (42 miles) Antipatris to Caesarea (26 miles)	Acts 23 – Paul was arrested in Jerusalem, sent to Antipatris, and then on to Caesarea to be presented to Felix the governor.
75 miles	Nazareth to Jerusalem (via Samaria)	Luke 2:41-52 – Jesus traveled with his parents every year to Jerusalem for the Feast of the Passover (the most direct route passed directly through the territory of Samaria).
80 miles	Bethlehem to Nazareth	Luke 2:1-7 – Joseph and Mary left Nazareth to be registered for the census in Bethlehem as decreed by Caesar Augustus.
97 miles	Nazareth to Jerusalem (via Jericho)	Luke 2:41-52 – In order to avoid walking through Samaria, Jews would take the long way, through Jericho, when traveling north from Jerusalem.
135 miles	Jerusalem to Damascus	Acts 9 – Saul was traveling the road from Jerusalem to Damascus with the intention of finding and imprisoning the Christians in that city—but the Lord had other plans for him.
250 miles	Goshen, Egypt to Canaan (the most direct route)	Exodus 13:17-18 – God did not lead his people along this route because it would take them through the land of the Philistines. He led them instead by way of the wilderness.

300 miles	Jerusalem to Antioch	Acts 11:22 – Barnabas left Jerusalem to encourage the believers in Antioch.
300 miles	Dothan to Egypt	Genesis 37:17-28 – Joseph was sold into slavery by his brothers in Dothan and was taken to the land of Egypt.
400 miles	Haran to Shechem	Genesis 12:4-6 – Abram departed from Haran and traveled to the Land of Canaan, stopping in Shechem to build an altar to the Lord.
550 miles	Jerusalem to Babylon	2 Chronicles 36:15-21 – This is the route traveled by the exiled Jews.
600 miles	Ur to Haran	Genesis 11:31 – Abram left Ur of the Chaldeans with his father, his nephew, and his wife and settled in Haran.

MILEAGE LOG

Keep track of your mileage and compare it to the list of Bible distances. Have you walked 3.5 miles? The Walls of Jericho have just come down! Have you logged 11 miles? Well, how long did it take for you to cross the Red Sea?

Sunday	Monday	Tuesday	Wednes-day	Thursday	Friday	Saturday	Weekly Total	Overall total
0	1	1	0	1.5	1.5	2	7	7

Sunday	Monday	Tuesday	Wednes-day	Thursday	Friday	Saturday	Weekly Total	Overall total
0	2	1	0	2	2	4	11	18

Sunday	Monday	Tuesday	Wednes-day	Thursday	Friday	Saturday	Weekly Total	Overall total

Sunday	Monday	Tuesday	Wednes-day	Thursday	Friday	Saturday	Weekly Total	Overall total

Sunday	Monday	Tuesday	Wednes-day	Thursday	Friday	Saturday	Weekly Total	Overall total

Sunday	Monday	Tuesday	Wednes-day	Thursday	Friday	Saturday	Weekly Total	Overall total

Sunday	Monday	Tuesday	Wednes-day	Thursday	Friday	Saturday	Weekly Total	Overall total

Sunday	Monday	Tuesday	Wednes-day	Thursday	Friday	Saturday	Weekly Total	Overall total
Sunday	Monday	Tuesday	Wednes-day	Thursday	Friday	Saturday	Weekly Total	Overall total
Sunday	Monday	Tuesday	Wednes-day	Thursday	Friday	Saturday	Weekly Total	Overall total
Sunday	Monday	Tuesday	Wednes-day	Thursday	Friday	Saturday	Weekly Total	Overall total
Sunday	Monday	Tuesday	Wednes-day	Thursday	Friday	Saturday	Weekly Total	Overall total
Sunday	Monday	Tuesday	Wednes-day	Thursday	Friday	Saturday	Weekly Total	Overall total
Sunday	Monday	Tuesday	Wednes-day	Thursday	Friday	Saturday	Weekly Total	Overall total
Sunday	Monday	Tuesday	Wednes-day	Thursday	Friday	Saturday	Weekly Total	Overall total
Sunday	Monday	Tuesday	Wednes-day	Thursday	Friday	Saturday	Weekly Total	Overall total

NAZARETH TO JORDAN RIVER | *50 Miles (Beginner)*

Jesus walked from Nazareth to the Jordan River to be baptized by John. (Mark 1:9)

Week	Sunday	Monday	Tuesday	Wednesday	Thursday	Friday	Saturday
1	CT or Rest	1 mile	1 mile	CT or Rest	1 mile	CT or Rest	1.5 miles
2	CT or Rest	1.5 miles	1.5 miles	CT or Rest	2 miles	CT or Rest	2 miles
3	CT or Rest	1.5 miles	1.5 miles	CT or Rest	2 miles	CT or Rest	2.5 miles
4	CT or Rest	2 miles	2.5 miles	CT or Rest	2.5 miles	CT or Rest	2.5 miles
5	CT or Rest	2.5 miles	2.5 miles	CT or Rest	2.5 miles	CT or Rest	3 miles
6	CT or Rest	2.5 miles	2.5 miles	CT or Rest	3 miles	CT or Rest	3 miles

CT or Rest: Use the day to rest or to do light Cross Training (CT) activities such as Calisthenics, Yoga, or Swimming

BETHLEHEM TO NAZARETH | *80 Miles (Intermediate)*

Joseph and Mary left Nazareth to be registered for the census in Bethlehem as decreed by Caesar Augustus. (Luke 2:1-7)

Week	Sunday	Monday	Tuesday	Wednesday	Thursday	Friday	Saturday
1	CT or Rest	2 miles	2 miles	CT or Rest	2.5 miles	CT or Rest	2.5 miles
2	CT or Rest	2.5 miles	3 miles	CT or Rest	3 miles	CT or Rest	3 miles
3	CT or Rest	3 miles	3 miles	CT or Rest	3 miles	CT or Rest	3 miles
4	CT or Rest	3 miles	3 miles	CT or Rest	3 miles	CT or Rest	4 miles
5	CT or Rest	4 miles	4 miles	CT or Rest	4 miles	CT or Rest	4.5 miles
6	CT or Rest	4 miles	4 miles	CT or Rest	5 miles	CT or Rest	5 miles

CT or Rest: Use the day to rest or to do light Cross Training (CT) activities such as Calisthenics, Yoga, or Swimming

JERUSALEM TO DAMASCUS | *135 Miles (Advanced)*

Saul was traveling the road from Jerusalem to Damascus with the intention of finding and imprisoning the Christians in that city--but the Lord had other plans for him! (Acts 9)

Week	Sunday	Monday	Tuesday	Wednesday	Thursday	Friday	Saturday
1	CT or Rest	3 miles	3 miles	CT or Rest	4 miles	3 miles	5 miles
2	CT or Rest	4 miles	4 miles	CT or Rest	5 miles	4 miles	5 miles
3	CT or Rest	4 miles	4 miles	CT or Rest	5 miles	4 miles	5 miles
4	CT or Rest	4 miles	4 miles	CT or Rest	5 miles	4 miles	5 miles
5	CT or Rest	4 miles	5 miles	CT or Rest	6 miles	4 miles	6 miles
6	CT or Rest	5 miles	5 miles	CT or Rest	6 miles	4 miles	6 miles

CT or Rest: Use the day to rest or to do light Cross Training (CT) activities such as Calisthenics, Yoga, or Swimming

40 DAY CHALLENGE

Challenge yourself to 40 straight days of activity. Select your favorite activity, or challenge yourself to try something new. Try to vary your intensity so your body can recover every couple days. Here are some suggestions: Walking, Jogging, Hiking, Cycling, Yoga, Stretching, Aerobics, Dancing, Weight Lifting, or Swimming.

Day 1	Day 2	Day 3	Day 4	Day 5	Day 6	Day 7	Day 8
Day 9	Day 10	Day 11	Day 12	Day 13	Day 14	Day 15	Day 16
Day 17	Day 18	Day 19	Day 20	Day 21	Day 22	Day 23	Day 24
Day 25	Day 26	Day 27	Day 28	Day 29	Day 30	Day 31	Day 32
Day 33	Day 34	Day 35	Day 36	Day 37	Day 38	Day 39	Day 40

100 REASONS TO EXERCISE

1. Reduces your risk of getting heart disease.

2. Increases your level of muscle strength.

3. Improves the functioning of your immune system.

4. Enhances sexual desire, performance, and satisfaction.

5. Helps you to more effectively manage stress.

6. Helps you to lose weight – especially fat weight.

7. Improves the likelihood of survival from a myocardial infarction (heart attack).

8. Can help relieve the pain of tension headaches.

9. Improves your body's ability to use fat for energy during physical activity.

10. Increases the density and breaking strength of your bones.

11. Helps to preserve lean body tissue.

12. Reduces the risk of developing hypertension (high blood pressure).

13. Increases the density and breaking strength of you ligaments and tendons.

14. Improves coronary (heart) circulation.

15. Increases circulating levels of HDL (good) cholesterol.

16. Assists in efforts to stop smoking.

17. Reduces your risk of developing Type II (non-insulin dependent) diabetes.

18. Can help improve short term memory in older individuals.

19. Helps to maintain weight loss.

20. Helps relieve many of the common discomforts of pregnancy.

21. Reduces your anxiety level.

22. Helps control blood pressure in people with hypertension.

23. Reduces the viscosity of your blood.

24. Reduces vulnerability to various cardiac dysrhythmias (abnormal heart rhythms).

25. Increases your maximal oxygen uptake.

26. Helps to overcome jet lag.

27. Slows the rate of joint degeneration in people with osteoarthritis.

28. Lowers your resting heart rate.

29. Helps to boost creativity.

30. Reduces circulating levels of triglycerides.

31. Helps the body resist upper respiratory tract infections.

32. Increases your anaerobic threshold, allowing you to exercise longer at a higher level before lactic acid build-up.

33. Reduces medical and healthcare expenses.

34. Improves ability to recover from physical exertion.

35. Helps speed the recovery from chemotherapy treatments.

36. Increases ability to supply blood to the skin for cooling.

37. Increases the thickness of the cartilage in your joints.

38. Gives you more energy to meet the demands of daily life, and provides a reserve for emergencies.

39. Increases your level of muscle endurance.

40. Helps you to sleep easier and better.

41. Improves posture.

42. Improves athletic performance.

43. Helps you to maintain your resting metabolic rate.

44. Reduces the risk of colon cancer.

45. Increases your tissues' responsiveness to the actions of insulin, helping to control blood sugar.

46. Helps to relieve constipation.

47. Expands blood plasma volume.

48. Reduces the risk of developing prostate cancer.

49. Helps to combat substance abuse.

50. Helps to alleviate depression.

51. Increases your ability to adapt to cold environments.

52. Helps you maintain proper muscle balance.

53. Reduces the rate and severity of medical complications associated with hypertension.

54. Helps to alleviate certain menstrual symptoms.

55. Lowers your heart rate response to submaximal physical exertion.

56. Helps to alleviate lower back pain.

57. Helps to reduce the amount of insulin required to control blood sugar levels in Type I diabetics.

58. Improves mental alertness.

59. Improves respiratory muscle strength and endurance – important for asthmatics.

60. Reduces your risk of having a stroke.

61. Helps you to burn excess calories.

62. Increases your cardiac reserve.

63. Improves your physical appearance.

64. Offsets some of the negative side-effects of certain antihypertensive drugs.

65. Increases your stroke volume (amount of blood the heart pumps each beat).

66. Improves your self-esteem.

67. Reduces your susceptibility for coronary thrombosis (clot in the artery that supplies blood to the heart).

68. Helps you to relax.

69. Reduces the risk of developing breast cancer.

70. Improves mental cognition (short term only).

71. Maintains or improves joint flexibility.

72. Improves your glucose tolerance.

73. Reduces workdays missed due to illness.

74. Protects against "creeping obesity" (slow, steady weight gain that occurs as you age).

75. Enhances your muscles' abilities to extract oxygen from your blood.

76. Increases your productivity at work.

77. Reduces your likelihood of developing low back problems.

78. Improves your balance and coordination.

79. Allows you to consume greater quantities of food and still maintain caloric balance.

80. Provides protection against injury.

81. Decreases (by 20-30%) the need for antihypertensive medication.

82. Improves your decision-making abilities.

83. Helps reduce and prevent the immediate symptoms of menopause and decreases the long-term risks of cardiovascular disease, osteoporosis, and obesity.

84. Helps to relieve and prevent "migraine headache attacks."

85. Reduces the risk of endometriosis (common cause of infertility).

86. Help to retard bone loss as you age, thereby reducing your risk of developing osteoporosis.

87. Helps decrease your appetite (short term only).

88. Improves pain tolerance and mood if you suffer from osteoporosis.

89. Helps prevent and relieve the stresses that cause carpal tunnel syndrome.

90. Makes your heart a more efficient pump.

91. Helps to decrease left ventricular hypertrophy (thickening of the wall of the left ventricle) in people with hypertension.

92. Improves your mood.

93. Helps to increase your overall health awareness.

94. Reduces the risk of gastrointestinal bleeding.

95. Helps you to maintain an independent lifestyle.

96. Reduces the risk of abdominal obesity – a significant health risk factor.

97. Increases the diffusion capacity of the lungs, enhances the exchange of oxygen from your lungs to your blood.

98. Improves heat tolerance.

99. Improves your overall quality of life.

100. Lifelong regular exercise may be protective against development of Alzheimer's disease.

Made in the USA
San Bernardino, CA
16 March 2017